THE SOCIAL HERBIVORE

PERFECT PAIRINGS FOR PLANT-BASED CUISINE

by Priya Rao & Jennifer Hue

Printed in Canada

First paperback edition September 2021

Cover Design by Danielle Adams
Interior Layout & Design by Sarah Carriere
Photography by Kat Rizza
Hair & Makeup by Shannon Leigh

ISBN 978-1-7778209-0-9

www.thesocialherbivore.co
@socialherbivore

Our book is about the pleasures of enjoying meals with loved ones, however we are aware that this is a privilege and that many people around the world experience food shortages and must rely on food banks.

We are proud to support the Toronto Vegetarian Food Bank (a volunteer-powered registered charity). In our shared belief that people should not be forced to compromise their health, or their ethics, when they are already in such a vulnerable position. That's why $1 from each book sold will go to the TVFB. To learn more about them, visit www.tvfb.ca

We want to thank you for picking up our book. By doing so you're helping more families enjoy laughter over the dinner table.

Photo taken at Karlo Estates, producers of the first vegan-certified wine in the world.

FOREWARD BY CHEF LESLIE DURSO

Dining is an experience! In this gorgeous book, Priya and Jennifer have created exactly that—a joyful celebration of food, wine and community. Every page launches a new culinary adventure.

I am Italian. I am a chef. And I am vegan. You might have guessed, then, that my favorite thing in this world is creating a food experience to share with others. This book inspires us all to do just that. Connection through food and wine is magical.

My ideal day? To sit in the garden of a special villa in Ravello, looking over the Mediterranean, hand-rolling pasta while a sauce made with produce picked from the hillside garden simmers in the kitchen. To know that soon, friends and I will open a bottle of lush red wine made of grapes grown from the same soil. We'll dine and talk into the wee hours as the moon casts its reflection on the water and conversation swirls through the air. And it will be an experience we call to mind from time to time, and smile.

In this book, Priya & Jennifer share memories and encourage us to create our own. For each delicious recipe, Priya evokes a moment in time that brings the food alive. For those new to the vegan lifestyle, or readers who are simply curious, these recipes show what is possible—to create food we crave that is good for our health and the planet.

Jennifer expands the conversation with a passion for wine that jumps off the page. She inspires us to expand our palate. Her vision for pairing wine with vegan cuisine is unparalleled. My favorite part: her suggestions for creating a tasting experience in which friends try similar wines and discuss the nuances. Those conversations start with the wine and lead to shared stories ... tales of travel, childhood memories, and simple, joyful moments.

Priya expands our consciousness about what is possible in vegan dining. Jennifer shows us that consciousness doesn't stop with our fork, offering education about clean wine.

Vegan food comes from the ground. So do the grapes that create the wine. What's not to love about food and wine? Invite friends into the mix, and it's the perfect recipe for an unforgettable experience.

WELCOME FROM PRIYA

I am so delighted that you're here! This book is a passion project that I first conceived of back in 2014 when I began to develop a keen interest in wine. It irked me that plant-based cuisine was left out of traditional conversations around food and wine pairing. We've all heard that 'red wine goes with red meat and white wine goes with white meat', but what goes best with a cashew-cream pasta, or a Mushroom Wellington? I am grateful to have Master Sommelier, Jen Huether as my partner in this endeavor.

I've been vegan for over a decade and was vegetarian for almost 15 years prior to that but I grew up eating meat and most of my favourite meals and comfort foods revolved around meat. That's why what we do at The Social Herbivore exists in a judgement-free zone. There is no guilt here for those who aren't looking to go completely vegan.

I am not a chef, what I am is a really good cook who loves to entertain. Good food and wine are like a campfire around which we gather with our friends and loved ones to share stories, experiences and laughter. That's why we've grouped our recipes around the conversations that occur at the table—Small Talk, Big Talk and Sweet Talk.

My hope is that no longer will hosts feel they need to make a separate dish for the vegan at their table, and no longer will non-vegans crinkle their noses at an invitation to a dinner party hosted by a vegan. These are dishes that everyone can enjoy together whether they are plant-based or not. Alongside Jen's fabulous wine pairings, our goal is to help you experience those magical taste explosions that occur when a wine and a dish meld perfectly together.

This book has been many years in the making and I hope you enjoy not only the recipes and pairings, but all the tips and info we've compiled to help make your family gatherings, romantic dinners and festive cocktail parties all the more special.

WELCOME FROM JENNIFER

Thank you so much for coming and joining us on our journey! This book has been a three year passion project for us and lots of love and time and learning has gone into it. In the following pages you will find some delicious recipes Priya has created that I have had the 'arduous' task of tasting and finding perfectly partnered wine pairings for, taking out all the guess work for you. I have included wines from differing price points, styles and countries so you can really take a trip around the world in a glass. Please have fun, explore and enjoy the experience. At the end of each pairing I offer tips and tricks to get the most enjoyment out of your pairing such as service temperatures and glassware. Beyond the pairings I offer you some of the most valuable information that I have learned in my two decades of being in the wine business.

It was five years ago that a friend suggested that I should focus on plant-based pairings. When her family (who are all vegan) would come over for dinner I would struggle to figure out a meal everyone would eat. I would make the classic spaghetti with faux meat sauce and find a bottle of red and hope it worked. She made me realize that there was so much to discover with plant-based food and wine. She inspired me to create a presentation, seminar, and dinner around plant-based food and wine, which is where I met Priya! Priya had had the idea to write this book for years, and after one conversation with her, I was in.

I have become more and more plant-based over the years for many reasons, including my love of animals, the environment, and for my health. However I don't want to feel like I am missing out on a great dining experience or the taste explosions that can occur when you find a perfect food and wine match. It's been a pleasure to continue to grow and learn in this space and a blessing to be working with Priya. I hope you enjoy creating and tasting!

WHAT DO VEGANS EAT?

Set your FOMO aside because there's no 'fear of missing out' in these pages!

The hardest part for me when I became vegan was giving up the meals I had grown up with. My go-to comfort foods were all about pie: shepherd's pie, pot pie, coconut cream pie, OH MY! How could it be that I would never enjoy these delicious foods again?

Fear not, as the collection of recipes in this book includes veganized versions of all the above pies! Every recipe was tested by non-vegans to ensure that they passed the taste test for those who don't consider themselves plant-based.

The main criteria for all recipes that made it into this book is that they shocked Jen and all the non-vegan friends who've eaten them in one of 2 ways:

1) they were completely fooled that the dishes did not contain meat

2) they deemed the dishes as good as, if not better than, the original meat-based recipes

In short, if you think vegan food is bland, boring and consists of salads and steamed vegetables, think again. I triple dog dare you not to be pleasantly surprised by these recipes!

I sense the skepticism and believe me, I understand it. The idea of giving up what has always been the centrepiece of your plate is daunting. We've become conditioned to think of 'protein' in animal terms—chicken, beef, and fish. It's been hammered into us from all sides and somehow we have forgotten that beans, legumes, nuts, seeds, vegetables, and yes, the much maligned tofu, are all great sources of clean protein.

"What will I eat?", you ask? You will eat Irish stew, mushroom risotto, creamy pasta, classic lasagna, crabless cakes, jackfruit sliders, chickpea 'tuna' pockets, mushroom wellington, sticky toffee pudding and so much more.

Knowing that many of you reading this book may be new to plant-based cuisine, or may simply be referring to it to find a recipe to welcome your son's girlfriend to dinner, this is a collection of traditional favourite dishes such as those mentioned above that have been veganized to make the transition less jarring. I use various faux meats in some recipes with options for those who prefer to avoid processed products and stick to whole foods.

You know how your parents give you the old, 'When I was young, I had to walk uphill both ways to school' speech? Well, I'm about to say something similar because when I became vegan, around 2010, the best we could expect from faux meat products was that they were rubbery OR tasteless, and not both.

Well, we've come a long way baby and today's veggie burgers, sausages and other faux meats are great-tasting alternatives to help add plant-based options to your diet in a seamless way. Important to note that moderation is a great skill to practice here, because most of those meat alternatives are usually high in fat and sodium.

What I'm trying to get at is that it's a lot easier today to add plant-based meals to your rotation. We've tried to assemble a variety of dishes in terms of flavour profiles, spices used, heat level and level of difficulty. There are recipes from various cultures--Thai, Italian, Greek, Vietnamese, Japanese, as well as continental dishes. It's a broad spectrum and with the vastness of tastes and flavours, you'll get a greater range of knowledge in terms of pairing wine with a variety of foods.

Jen's wine pairings will take you on a similar journey and include wines from most of the wine regions around the world, and many grape varietals, both popular and lesser known.

Ready to get your taste buds tingling? Let's go!

Note: *A couple of quick tips before you get cooking. Always read the recipe fully before you start making the dish, and try to gather and measure your ingredients so you don't accidentally forget to add a spice or possibly add it twice!*

SMALL TALK

A great meal often starts leisurely and gains momentum as the courses come out. Guests are milling around, greeting one another and catching up with casual conversation. Here is a collection of appetizers, hors d'oeuvres and first courses to help set the stage for all parties—dinner or cocktail.

CRABBY CAKES WITH TARTAR SAUCE

Makes 20 appetizer size cakes

I promised in the introduction that a lot of the recipes will be veganized versions of classic, popular dishes. I present to you the vegan crab cake with a homemade sauce that will make your guests do a double take to confirm that they are, in fact, vegan! The trick is the seaweed and the Old Bay seasoning which simulate those sea flavours. These are great as a starter course, or you could make them even smaller and serve as a finger food with a dollop of the tartar sauce on top.

TARTAR SAUCE

1/2 cup vegan mayonnaise

1 tbsp chopped pickle

1/4 cup chopped fresh dill

CRABBY CAKES

1 x 19 oz can chickpeas

1 x 15 oz can hearts of palm

1 x 8 oz jar marinated artichoke hearts, drained (liquid reserved)

1 cup breadcrumbs plus an extra 3/4 cup for coating

1/2 cup vegan mayonnaise divided into 2 equal portions

1 tsp Dijon mustard

2 tsp lemon juice

1 tbsp Old Bay seasoning

1 sheet nori or other seaweed, crumbled

1 tbsp chopped, fresh dill

Salt & pepper to taste

Oil, for frying

MAKE THE TARTAR SAUCE

Combine vegan mayonnaise, chopped pickle and dill in a mixing bowl and stir well to combine. Refrigerate until ready to serve.

MAKE THE CAKES

Pulse chickpeas, hearts of palm, and artichoke hearts in a food processor several times, keeping an eye on the texture. Mixture should be chunky, not minced.

Transfer mixture to a large bowl. Add 1 cup bread crumbs, 1/4 cup vegan mayonnaise, Dijon mustard, 1 teaspoon lemon juice, Old Bay seasoning and seaweed. Taste before adding salt and pepper. Mix well. Refrigerate for at least 30 minutes to help the mixture hold together when forming patties.

Once the mixture has cooled, form it into 1 inch thick patties about 2 inches in diameter.

Heat 1 tbsp oil in a non-stick pan. Coat each patty in remaining bread crumbs and fry until golden brown, about 3-5 minutes per side, adding 1 tablespoon of oil per batch of cakes.

Top the cakes with tartar sauce, sprinkle with chopped dill, and serve with a wedge of lemon.

It is unreal how delicious and similar these are in comparison to the original dish they are representing. That two-ingredient tartar sauce - really divine!

My value pick is a dry Chenin Blanc from South Africa. These wines are intriguing and can be slightly herbal with lots of lemon tartness, pear and passion fruit notes. Zippy acidity helps contrast the richness of the fried bread crumb crust and creamy tartar sauce and makes for a unique pairing.

My splurge is taking the Chenin Blanc grape back to its origins in the Loire Valley, France. Here the beautiful, elegant and dry expression of this grape hits its pinnacle with the wines from Savennières. These white wines somehow have the ability to be mouth filling and refreshing, at the same time. Expect more notes of chamomile, apple blossom, hay and quince. This match could be one of my all-time favorites for either spring or summer.

Pro Tip: *Savennières can age and improve for 5-10 years so buy an extra bottle for the cellar.*

Smashed Chickpea Salad Pockets (Page 18), Jalapeño Finger Poppers (Page 19)

ASIAN MAD-FOR-MUSHROOM WRAPS

Makes 10-12 buffet-style wraps

So many appetizers revolve around dough of some kind, whether it's crackers, bread or pastry. This is a great alternative that is super tasty, yet light and healthy. Mushrooms are already low-calorie and stocked with protein, antioxidants, potassium and fibre. To get the most from this nutrition-packed veggie, try to incorporate as many types of mushrooms as you can find.

2 tbsp coconut or olive oil

1 large red onion, sliced

4 cups mixed mushrooms, sliced to roughly the same size

2 tbsp vegetarian hoisin sauce (found at most Asian grocery stores)

2 tbsp soy sauce

3-4 tbsp water

4-6 cloves garlic, minced

1 small Thai red chili, finely sliced (seeds removed for a less spicy version)

1 tbsp ginger, minced

1 tbsp rice wine vinegar

1 tbsp sesame oil

2 green onions, white and light green portions sliced

1 head iceberg lettuce, leaves carefully separated

Heat oil in a wok or large frying pan over medium-high heat. Add red onion and mushrooms and cook for 5-7 minutes until the mushrooms have released their moisture and it has cooked off.

In a small bowl combine hoisin sauce, soy sauce, water, garlic, red chili, ginger and vinegar. Add to mushrooms and cook until absorbed. Mixture should be slightly saucy.

Remove from heat and mix in the sesame oil and green onions.

Serve alongside lettuce leaves, allowing guests to build their own wraps.

I am in love with this gluten free and delicious appetizer option. We had a lot of fun matching this dish as well! There was lots of natural umami from the cooked mushrooms which lent itself really nicely to wine. My value pick is a white wine, a New Zealand Pinot Gris from the Marlborough region. A refreshing and lively Pinot Gris makes the dish sparkle while the weight and texture of the wine plays off the density of the mushrooms. Pinot Gris can lend itself to earthy, mushroom notes as well which aids in this match.

For my splurge wine, I am going to France in the region of Beaujolais suggesting an elevated Cru. Cru Beaujolais is based on the Gamay grape and is generally more complex and earthy than the more value-driven non-Cru Beaujolais on the market. There are 10 different villages which have this special designation of Cru so you can play around with the different ones; however, be sure to try something from the Village Morgon at some point. This gamay has mouth-watering acidity that's coupled with dusty, earthy notes and tannins that are not too overbearing. The earthy notes marry so well with the mushrooms that it seems to be a match made in heaven while the acid in the wine offers some refreshment to this dish.

Pro Tip: *Serve the Beaujolais Cru slightly chilled and in big glasses (like Burgundy Glasses).*

SMASHED CHICKPEA SALAD POCKETS

Makes 20 servings

Have I mentioned that I love finger foods as appetizers? Then I've also said the reason I love them is that they don't require plates and therefore make cleanup a cinch. This is yet another example of the versatility of the common chickpea. Truly an amazing and amazingly affordable source of protein and fibre, there is so much goodness packed into this small legume! If you miss tuna salad, this may turn into your new go-to lunch.

1 x 19 oz can chickpeas, drained

1/3 cup vegan mayo

I baby pickle, finely diced

1/4 cup each celery and carrot, thinly sliced

1/4 cup green or red onion, finely diced (optional)

1 tsp pickle (or marinated artichoke) juice

1/2 to 1 large sheet of nori (seaweed) crumbled

1/2 tsp Old Bay Seasoning

1/4 tsp mustard

1 tsp lemon juice

Salt & pepper to taste

10 mini pita pockets cut in half or sliced cucumbers

In a small pot, steam the chickpeas for 2-3 minutes to slightly soften them. Drain, blanch with cold water and let cool completely.

In a medium sized bowl, mash the chickpeas with a fork or a potato masher until there are no big pieces, but it's not quite mush. Transfer chickpeas to a bowl, and add remaining ingredients, mixing until well combined.

Cool the salad in the refrigerator for at least an hour for flavours to meld together.

Serve in mini pita pockets or on top of sliced cucumbers for a low-carb and fully raw finger food.

This works with a variety of wines, but a crisp Chardonnay is the way to go especially if you're not adding bread.

My value pick is a Chardonnay from the Niagara region in Ontario, Canada. If you go full-on fancy with the sandwich, you could choose a French-style, oaky Chardonnay to compliment the richness of the chosen bread. If you are going with a thinner and lighter bread, for example tortillas or pitas, choose an un-oaked light and delicate style of Chardonnay. Ontario makes both very well.

For my splurge pick, I would head to the famed Napa Valley for an iconic California Chardonnay. These wines tend to be full throttle, with a rich finish and a creamy texture. They work very well with a dense white French Baguette. This is a surprising match but there is both saltiness and richness in this sandwich. I recommend cutting them into little fancy 'High tea' type servings for that extra "wow" effect.

Pro Tip: *Don't overchill your good Chardonnay as you will lose all the lovely nuances in the glass.*

JALAPEÑO FINGER POPPERS

Makes 12 poppers

Another fun finger food with a cheesy stuffing! Since not all jalapeños are created equal, you may have a couple with no heat and then be hit with a punch! I find that surprise to be quite enjoyable and it's the heat that makes the wine pairing so excellent but if you want to avoid the burn, make sure you remove all the seeds and membranes from the peppers.

6 large jalapeños, sliced lengthwise in half, seed and membranes removed

1 medium potato, diced

1/2 cup raw cashews

1 tsp olive oil

1 small onion, diced

2 cloves garlic, minced

2 tbsp nutritional yeast

2 tsp white miso paste

1/2 tsp cumin

1/2 to 3/4 cup vegetable broth

2 tsp chipotle in adobo sauce

Crushed nacho chips for topping

Heat the oven to 400 °F.

Pre-bake jalapeños for 5 minutes until softened.

Steam potato in a small pot of slightly salted water for 5-7 mins until soft. Add cashews in for the last 2 mins.

Meanwhile, heat the oil in a small frying pan over medium heat and cook the onion and garlic for 5-7 minutes.

Add potatoes, cashews, onion and garlic blend, nutritional yeast, miso paste, cumin, half a cup of the vegetable broth, and the chipotle to a blender and blend until smooth. Add more broth slowly, if needed. Mixture will be thick, creamy and slightly sticky from the starch in the potatoes.

Spoon the mixture into the peppers, being careful not to have them overflow. Top with crushed nachos.

Bake for 15 minutes until the peppers are soft and the filling is slightly browned.

This is an interesting and contrasting dish. There is some heat from the jalapeño itself, there is also crunch and salt from the nacho chips on top which adds great texture.

My value pick is Moscato d'Asti from Piedmont in Northern Italy. With around 5.5% alcohol and a floral, delicate freshness, this is a dream match. It also has some sweetness which counteracts those spicy bites, and the bubbles make it a festive match.

My splurge pick is an off-dry German Deutscher Sekt from any region. Sekt is the German word for sparkling wine and is one of Germany's best kept secrets (they tend to drink most of it in Germany). The sweetness helps temper the spice and brings some coolness to your palate to counteract the heat. Again, we don't want anything with too much alcohol or it's going to bring the heat out even more. These wines are crowd pleasers, and with this wine you may be able to introduce something totally new to your guests.

Pro Tip: *Have fun with the glassware here. Antique, oddly shaped sparkling glasses or aperitif glasses add to the fun of this appetizer course.*

SPINACH ARTICHOKE DIP

Serves 6-8

The classic of classics! This is better than any store-bought dip. Plus it's a perfect party appetizer since it's served in a bowl of bread, so no cleanup. However, if you want a lower-carb option you can serve it in a bowl with some fresh veggies and bread on the side.

1 tbsp olive oil

1 medium onion, chopped

4 cloves garlic, minced

1/2 tsp red chili flakes

1 bunch spinach (or a 5 oz package) roughly chopped

1 x 420 g package soft or regular tofu

1 x 12 oz jar marinated artichoke hearts, roughly chopped, marinade reserved separately

1 tsp dried oregano

1 1/2 tsp salt

1/2 cup nutritional yeast

1/4 cup vegan mayonnaise

1 round loaf of sourdough or pumpernickel bread

Preheat the oven to 350 °F.

Heat oil in a medium skillet over medium heat. Add onions and sauté until soft, about 4-5 minutes. Add garlic and crushed chili flakes, if using. Reduce heat to low and cook for another minute being careful that the garlic doesn't burn. Add spinach and cook just until wilted.

Add tofu, artichoke marinade, oregano and salt to a food processor or mini-chopper. Process for 30-45 seconds until smooth. Add the spinach mixture and nutritional yeast, pulsing 10-15 times but be careful not to overblend.

Transfer to a mixing bowl, add the chopped artichokes and mayonnaise and stir well. Season with more salt if needed.

Transfer to a small casserole dish and bake for 25-30 minutes. Serve inside a hollowed out pumpernickel loaf or in the casserole dish with the veggies and bread on the side.

This is a great way to start off a meal and can have your crew nibbling as you work on dinner. A Riesling is your best bet here and anything from a dry Riesling to a sweeter one will work depending on how much chili flakes you're adding to the recipe. Look to Germany's Mosel region for off-dry styles with zippy acidity if you have increased the heat. Alternatively, Washington State has some excellent and sturdy Riesling in dry to slightly off-dry styles that will amaze. Riesling will help cut through the creaminess of this dish without overpowering the delicate flavours.

Pro Tip: *German Rieslings from the Mosel region come in off-dry and low alcohol versions and there's no need to break the bank on them. Starting off with a lighter wine is a lovely way to begin a meal and does not overpower the next course or give you palate fatigue. Rieslings are one of my favourite aperitif wines.*

CREAMY CORN CHOWDER

Serves 4-6

I usually think of soup as a fall/winter dish but when Mother Nature gives you a bounty of corn, you've got to get creative because there are only so many steamed or grilled ears of corn you can eat! This soup is filling enough to be a meal on its own, or serve in smaller portions as a first course to your late summer dinner party.

1 tbsp olive oil

1 small red onion, chopped

3 cloves garlic, sliced

1/4 cup dry white wine

1 medium potato, peeled and diced

1 1/2-2 tsp black salt (found in Indian grocery stores or in bulk food stores)

Black pepper

3 ears corn, kernals sliced off, about 1 1/2 cups (reserve 1/4 cup)

2 cups vegetable broth

2 cups unsweetened almond milk

2 tbsp nutritional yeast

1/4 tsp dried parsley

2 tbsp nutritional yeast

1/2 cup canned coconut milk (preferably the solid, cream portion)

Fresh parsley and/or croutons for garnish

Heat oil in a large pot over medium heat.

Sauté red onion and garlic for 2-3 minutes, until soft. Add wine and cook until absorbed. Add potato and season with 1 1/2 teaspoons of the black salt and a few grinds of pepper. Taste and add remaining black salt if desired. Add all but the reserved 1/4 cup of corn, broth and almond milk. Bring to a boil, then reduce heat to a simmer and cook for another 5-7 minutes until potatoes are soft.

Transfer to a blender or use a hand blender and blend until smooth, or leave a few chunks for texture, if preferred.

Return to the pot and add coconut cream, nutritional yeast and remaining corn kernels. Cook for another 8-10 minutes until thickened. Serve with a sprig of parsley or some croutons on top.

Note: *Craving corn soup in the middle of winter? Using frozen or canned kernels works just as well!*

This tastes like August in a dish to me. Bursting with flavour and richness, and of course, corn notes!

My value pick is a Chardonnay from Santa Barbara in sunny Southern California, USA. These wines are intense and creamy with, at times, a hint of tropical fruit, but finish fresh thanks to the cool ocean breezes they encounter. Chardonnay matches well with this soup because like the soup, it usually has a creamy texture and weight to it. Chardonnays can also sometimes display notes of fresh or canned corn.

For my splurge wine I am going to go to Burgundy, France for a delicious Chardonnay from the Cote d'Or (aka 'slopes of gold'). There is no limit to what you can spend on top whites from this region, however I do find lots of value from the village of Beaune or Savigny-Lès-Beaune. These whites have a beautiful mineral edge and creamy, buttery texture that taste and work beautifully with this chowder.

Pro Tip: *This is a fun experiment of matching weight, texture and flavors in the wine with similarities in the dish. Close your eyes and experience heightened senses of smell and taste with this pairing.*

BOUGIE POTATO LEEK SOUP WITH GREMOLATA

Serves 4-6

We've all had potato leek soup but this book is about 'elevating' so let's take it up a notch, shall we? The gremolata is a great way to liven up what is an otherwise hearty, but rather simple and rustic soup. It's also a way to elevate your presentation. Amazing what a bit of minced garlic and parsley can do for a dish!

SOUP

2 tbsp olive oil

1 bunch leeks, roughly chopped

2 cloves garlic, chopped

1/4 cup dry white wine

2 large white potatoes, peeled & cubed

1 medium parsnip, chopped

4 cups vegetable broth

1 small bay leaf

1/2 tsp dried thyme

1/2 tsp salt

Black pepper to taste, approx. 1/4 tsp

1/4 cup canned coconut cream

GREMOLATA

1/2 cup loosely packed parsley

1 clove garlic

1 medium lemon, zested and juiced

1 tbsp olive oil

Salt & pepper to taste

Heat oil in a large frying pan over medium heat. Cook leeks and garlic for 2 minutes. Add wine and cook for another 5 minutes. Add potatoes, parsnip, broth, bay leaf, thyme salt and pepper. Cover and bring to a boil. Reduce heat and simmer, slightly covered, for 15-18 minutes until potatoes and parsnip are tender. Remove from heat.

In the meantime make the gremolata by mincing the parsley and garlic together. Add lemon zest and continue to mince until well blended. Transfer to a small bowl and add lemon juice, olive oil, salt and a pinch of black pepper. Too much pepper can overwhelm the parsley.

Remove the bay leaf from the pot, then purée the soup with a handheld blender or in an upright blender until smooth. Return soup to the pot, adding in the coconut cream and bring to a simmer for 2-3 minutes. Taste and adjust seasoning with salt and pepper.

Garnish soup with a drizzle of gremolata just before serving.

This soup certainly has a fresh and spring-like vibe to it and is quite pretty. Feel free to jazz it up a bit by drizzling the Gremolata in a fancy pattern for your guests. While potatoes on their own are dense and fairly neutral, the Gremolata adds lots of green, zesty flavours that match well with certain wines.

For my value pick I am going to Portugal for a lively little wine you may have never tried, Vinho Verde. This wine region is located in the Northwest of the country and has a moderate climate. White Vinho Verdes are high on acid and low on alcohol (between 8-11.5%), so they make an excellent aperitif wine and traditionally have a slight sparkle to them.

My splurge would be an Albariño from just across the border in Spain. This has become a fashionable grape in Spain and like its partner, Vinho Verde, it's high in acidity and provides citrus and stone fruit flavours, often with some salinity in the wine. It works so well with many foods and there are different price points, but I would recommend splurging a bit.

Pro Tip: *Since neither wine is overly expensive, buy both and have a side-by-side tasting experiencing this same grape from neighbouring countries! Both can handle the greenness of the Gremolata.*

SAFFRON-SCENTED ITALIAN WEDDING SOUP

Serves 4-6

I first made this soup on a cool spring evening. I had been waiting to get a new fridge and stove delivered and was trying to empty out my freezer. I decided to try a meatless version of Italian Wedding Soup. It. Was. Yummmm! I usually like big, bold flavours and lots of spices in my food, but the delicate, fragrant flavours of this hearty soup were exactly what that rainy Saturday called for.

2 tbsp olive oil + 1 tbsp for the meatballs

1 bag meatless meatballs of choice

2 large leeks, sliced (avoid the tough, dark green parts of the stalk)

2-3 cloves garlic, sliced

6 cups vegetable stock

1 large carrot, thinly sliced

1 can white kidney or navy beans, drained and rinsed

1 bunch spinach, roughly chopped

1/2 teaspoon packed saffron

Salt

Baguette, sliced

Vegan Parmesan (optional)

Heat oil in a medium frying pan over medium heat. Sauté the meatballs until lightly browned on all sides, approximately 8-10 minutes. Set aside.

Heat the remaining 2 tbsp olive oil in a large pot. Add leeks and sauté on medium heat for about 3 minutes until they start to soften. Add garlic and cook for another minute being careful not to burn the garlic or it will get bitter.

Add vegetable stock and carrots and cook until carrots are tender, about 8 minutes. Add meatballs, beans, spinach and saffron. Cook another minute or two to let flavours combine. Add salt to taste (depending on how salty your broth is).

Serve with a baguette and vegan parmesan, if using.

This soup is such a lovely bowl of goodness and savouriness, all while being very delicate.

My value pick is a surprising match. I'm opting to recommend a Torrontés from the Salta region in Argentina. These wines can be very floral and delicate, which is what makes this pairing surprising. This region's high altitude (highest vineyards in the world) produces unique whites from the Torrontés grape that are graceful and finish super fresh. This wine works so well because it's also delicate and aromatic just like this pretty soup.

My splurge pick is not necessarily a splurge but something perhaps new to you. I really like the white Fiano grape from Campania, Italy with this soup. These wines are generally nutty and heavily textured with floral notes and hints of spice and tropical fruit. Look for the famed 'Fiano di Avellino DOCG' wine when you're shopping. These wines are delicate enough to work with the soup but weighty enough to add a different dimension.

Pro Tip: *Matching hot liquid to cold liquid can be an interesting contrast. Play around with the temperatures of the wine to see different results.*

OLD-SCHOOL STUFFED MUSHROOMS

Makes 20 caps

Here's another dish that's been around seemingly since the dawn of time, or at least since the 1970s! And it has survived the decades because it's such a simple yet hearty finger food. When I'm hosting a party I particularly love food that's easy and mess-free so an appetizer you can pick off a platter and pop in your mouth is simply perfect!

3 tbsp olive oil (keep 1 tbsp separate)

1 large onion, diced

2 celery stalks, finely chopped

2 large carrots, finely chopped

1/4 cup dry white wine or vegetable broth

3 cloves garlic, minced

1/4 tsp salt

1 tsp Herbes de Provence

1 tbsp vegan parmesan or shredded mozzarella

1/2 cup panko bread crumbs

2 tbsp balsamic vinegar

1/4 tsp salt

Black pepper to taste

20 large cremini or white mushrooms (stems removed and diced)

Vegan parmesan

Preheat the oven to 350 °F.

Heat 1 tbsp oil in a large pan. Add onion, celery and carrots, cooking for 5 minutes. Add wine/broth and mushroom stems and cook for another 5 minutes. Add garlic, salt and Herbes de Provence and cook until soft. Add in a few twists of pepper from your pepper mill.

While the vegetables are cooking, blend remaining 2 tbsp olive oil and balsamic vinegar in a small bowl. Season with salt and pepper. Brush inside of mushroom caps with the balsamic mixture and bake for 5 minutes. Remove them from the oven.

Remove vegetables from heat. Add the vegan parmesan/mozzarella and bread crumbs. If needed, add extra salt and pepper. If the mixture is too wet, add more bread crumbs,
1 teaspoon at a time.

Stuff mushrooms with vegetable mixture and place on a baking sheet. Bake for 15-18 minutes.

Serve topped with a sprinkle of vegan parmesan.

An oldie but goodie here with this dish! I remember my Grandma serving these as bites prior to dinner. They still work today and can be used as a side dish or an appetizer. In either case, it's very fun to pair with some vino.

For my value pick I have chosen a white Greek Assyrtiko (ah-sir-tee-ko) from the fabulous island of Santorini. First off, this wine is so cool because it comes from one of the most iconic islands in the world. Second, it's delicious, mineral laden and bone dry with citrus vibes making it a great aperitif wine with a story to share.

For my splurge wine I am going with a Clare Valley Riesling from South Australia. This is a specialty of the region, and the vines are grown at an altitude which helps them become extremely zippy and fresh when young, while still showcasing a steely, mineral edge. Tart, citrus and racy acidity cleans off your palate and gets you ready for another bite. Both of these wines are great aperitif wine choices!

Pro Tip: *Try to find aged Clare Valley Riesling if you can, as with maturity, they develop wonderful honey notes!*

ELEGANT LEEK & ONION TART

Serves 8-10

Who doesn't like a warm and savoury tart? It's such a classy appetizer and a welcome change from chips and salsa. Plus the flavours are so delicate, which makes for a perfect pairing with the right glass of wine. Even better? It's super quick and easy to put together. While I like to serve small slices as finger foods, you could use the topping in a pie crust for a satisfyingly light dinner, served with a green salad in a zesty vinaigrette.

- 2 tbsp olive oil
- 2 medium white onions, thinly sliced
- 3 medium leeks, cleaned and sliced (white parts only)
- 1/4 cup dry or off-dry white wine
- 2 tsp Herbes de Provence or a blend of equal parts thyme, marjoram, rosemary and parsley
- 3/4 -1 tsp salt
- One package vegan-friendly puff pastry, thawed according to package instructions
- Pinch of black pepper to taste

Heat the oven to 425 °F.

Heat the olive oil In a large frying pan over medium-high heat. Cook onions and leeks until softened, about 3-5 minutes. Add wine and cook approximately 10-12 minutes or until the onions and leeks are caramelized. Season with Herbes de Provence, salt and pepper.

Roll out the puff pastry on a baking sheet. Spread topping evenly across pasty and crimp the edges. Bake for 15-17 minutes (depending on how hot your oven runs) until the edges and the underside of the pastry are golden brown.

Slice into small rectangles.

There is such a lovely sweetness from the caramelized onions and leeks, and the fluffy puffed pastry adds not only texture, but a bit more sweetness as well.

My value pick would be a dry Rosé from your local wine region. Rosé is incredibly versatile and food friendly, and dry styles can be found from around the world and are excellent with the crispy nature of the crust.

My splurge recommendation would also be a Rosé, but here I'm suggesting to go directly to the source of excellent dry Rosé, Provence in Southern France. It can certainly be easy to spend some green on the top examples from this region, but they are a lovely treat. Everything from the herbs to the caramelized onions and crispy crust balance in a lovely way with these exceptional and mouth-watering Rosés.

Pro Tip: *While certain Rosés can age and improve, I generally like to drink mine within two years of vintage.*

JERKY TOFU BITES

Makes 20-30 bites

I don't do too many 'raw' dishes but this is such an easy, make-ahead appetizer with loads of flavour. I know a lot of you probably detest tofu because it has 'no flavour', but the beauty of tofu is exactly that--it is a blank slate that is ready and waiting to soak up whatever seasoning you want to give it. This appetizer makes a very pretty plate once you top each tofu cube with colourful bell peppers.

One package extra firm tofu

3 green onions, chopped

4 large garlic cloves, chopped

1 small onion, chopped

4 to 5 small Thai red chilis, stemmed and seeded

2 tbsp fresh lime juice

2 tbsp soy sauce

3 tbsp olive oil

1 tbsp molasses

1 tbsp fresh thyme leaves (or 1 tsp dried)

2 tsp ground allspice

1 tsp ground black pepper

3/4 tsp freshly grated nutmeg

1/2 tsp cinnamon

1 tsp fresh ginger, grated

Salt (to taste, depending on how salty your soy sauce is)

Garnish: chopped bell peppers in a variety of colours

Slice tofu into half, width-wise, so you have two long slabs. Prick tofu with a toothpick throughout the surface so sauce can soak through.

Mix all ingredients (except the tofu) in a blender for about a minute. Pour over tofu. Marinate for about 2-3 hours in the refrigerator, flipping the tofu after an hour or so. Cut into cubes and top with the multi-coloured bell peppers, speared with a toothpick.

Note: *For a spicier marinade substitute Jalapeño or Scotch Bonnet peppers but adjust the amount accordingly as Thai red peppers are quite tiny in comparison.*

This has both types of heat, one from the spices and one from the Thai chillies. My value pick would be a Chenin Blanc from South Africa that works surprising well. South Africa is known for its beautiful and mineral driven fresh Chenin. While most Chenin Blanc from South Africa is dry, this dish brings out the sweetness in the wine and makes the wine sing, allowing the wine to stand up to the intense flavours of the jerk tofu.

My splurge pick would be a Sparkling wine from Spain. There are versions that come in at 11% alcohol and generally these sparkling wines are a bit more robust in body and texture than a Champagne, helping to combat the heat, yet working with the texture of the dish. With heat you always want to avoid high alcohol wines because this can elevate the sensation of heat in the dish.

Pro Tip: *Adjust the heat to your preferred style. If you do go very spicy, look for low alcohol and off-dry styles of wine to combat it. This dish is also great with beer!*

BIG TALK

Everyone is settled in and smiling. The atmosphere is amicable, and convivial. Now is the time when appetites are ready for the main course, and the bigger, dinner conversations. This collection of dishes provides options for buffet-style meals as well as plated ones. Sit back and enjoy as laughter fills one corner while a debate gains momentum in another! Set the mood with a playlist appropriate to the occasion or the dish, perhaps some opera for an Italian meal, jazz for an elegant dinner party, or classic pop and rock jams for an outdoor lunch.

MUSHROOM RISOTTO

Serves 4-6

The best mushroom risotto I ever had was during a bus tour of Italy at a random truck stop. It was so rich and creamy, and I thought I'd have to say goodbye to that type of experience once I became vegan but the fates had decided otherwise. The beauty of arborio rice is that it is inherently creamy so the longer you cook it, the creamier it becomes so I guarantee you won't miss the dairy in this version.

Note: *Risotto is finicky, like a high-maintenance woman. You have to nurture her, give her your undivided attention and you absolutely cannot rush her or she'll make you pay. So flex those wrists because they have a lot of stirring ahead!*

MUSHROOM BLEND

1 tbsp olive oil

1 large onion, chopped

4-6 cups mixed mushrooms, roughly chopped (the more variety the better)

4-6 cloves garlic, minced

1/4 cup red wine (*see note below)

1/2 tsp Herbes de Provence

Salt & pepper

RISOTTO

1 tbsp olive oil

2-3 medium shallots, finely chopped

1 cup arborio rice

1/4 cup white wine (*see note below)

3-4 cups vegetable broth

Salt & pepper

Optional: Truffle oil and vegan parmesan for garnish

MAKE THE MUSHROOMS

Heat oil in a medium pot over medium heat. Cook onions for 2-3 minutes. Add mushrooms and cook another 3-5 minutes until mushrooms have softened a bit. Add garlic and red wine, cooking until wine has evaporated. Add Herbes de Provences and stir until well mixed. Season with salt & pepper and remove from heat.

MAKE THE RISOTTO

Heat oil in a medium pot over medium heat. Cook shallots until soft, about 3 minutes. Lower heat to medium low, add risotto and stir just until rice is coated in oil. Add white wine and cook until liquid is almost completely soaked up and streaks the bottom of the pan. The rice should never actually stick to the pan. Add broth half a cup at a time following the same method above, stirring often but not constantly. Lower heat slightly if the liquid absorbs too quickly and sticks to the bottom of the pot.

Cooking time and amount of broth used will vary depending on whether you prefer your risotto a bit al dente (less broth + less time) or creamier (more broth + more time), but will roughly take 15-20 minutes. When it's reached your desired consistency, remove from heat and stir in the mushroom mixture. Season with salt, pepper and the truffle oil, if using, for more intense flavour. You could also drizzle truffle oil on top before serving.

Note: *This recipe is unusual because I use both red and white wine in it. White wine is preferred for the risotto portion, as red wine would impart a dark colour onto the rice. But I prefer red wine when cooking mushrooms because it results in a richer taste overall.*

Adding the mushrooms into the Risotto allows us to venture off into more umami rich red wines. For my value pick I am going to the sunny Sardinian Island with a Cannonau di Sardegna DOC. This is a lighter red wine based on the Cannonau grape and these wines can display colours of garnet and notes of soft red fruits, dusty tannins and an earthiness that is unique. They work so well with the earthiness of the mushrooms.

For my splurge pick, I am going to Spain with another warm and sunny region, Ribera del Douro. Here, we find hearty red wines based on the Tempranillo grape. Red wines are often blended here with here with other red Bordeaux varietals bought over by French winemakers. Look out for wines with age such as Reserva or Gran Reserva levels which denote 3 and 5 years of extra ageing, at a minimum. These iconic reds are sturdy, earthy and very complex and could certainly use a decant for a few hours prior to serving with the Risotto.

Pro Tip: *The high-quality wines of Ribera del Douro will age and improve even further in your cellar, so buy an extra bottle or two.*

LEMONY RISOTTO WITH SPRING GREENS

Serves 4

My go-to risotto in the fall has mushrooms, but as we crawl out of winter, I prefer a risotto with veggies that scream 'spring is here!' And you can't get more 'spring' than tender asparagus and fresh peas. The lemon zest is what gives this dish it's spark and brightness. It's a perfect meal for those slightly cool evenings as the days start to get just a bit longer.

2 tbsp olive oil

1 large shallot or small onion, diced

1 cup arborio rice

1/4 cup dry white wine

3-4 cups vegetable broth

Salt & pepper

1 bunch asparagus, chopped into 1 inch pieces

1/2 cup fresh peas

Zest and juice from a small lemon

Salt & pepper

Vegan parmesan (optional)

Heat 1 tbsp of the oil in a medium pot and cook shallot/onion on medium heat until soft, about 3 minutes. Add risotto and stir just until rice is coated in oil. Add white wine and cook until liquid is almost completely soaked up and streaks the bottom of the pan (note that the rice should never actually stick to the pan).

Add broth, half a cup at a time, following the same method above, stirring often but not constantly.

Cooking time and amount of broth used will vary depending on whether you prefer your risotto a bit al dente (less broth + less time) or creamier (more broth + more time), but will roughly take 15-20 minutes.

Meanwhile heat remaining oil in a medium fry pan. Cook asparagus for 3-4 minutes until you see the green turn brighter. Add peas and cook another minute, then season with salt and pepper.

When the risotto has reached your desired consistency, remove from heat and stir in the greens, lemon zest and lemon juice, 1 tablespoon at a time, tasting as you go so it doesn't get overly tart. Adjust taste with extra salt & pepper and serve with vegan parmesan on the side, if using.

Note: *Always serve risotto immediately as it will get mushy if it sits too long in the pot.*

The great thing about Risotto is that it's a fantastic vehicle for every other ingredient, sort of like pasta! This dish is devised with spring in mind and the ingredients that spring gives us (feel free to add fresh chives to it also).

My value pick wine is a Chilean Sauvignon Blanc from Casablanca Valley. First of all, Casablanca is my all-time favourite movie so there is that, but this is also a cool growing region for Chile, literally and figuratively! These crunchy and zesty whites have hints of green notes which meld perfectly with all the green things in this dish. The lemon notes and zesty acidity cut through the richness and weight of the dish, keeping it light and spring-like!

My splurge would be the same white grape variety, but from France. Look for either Sancerre or Pouilly-Fumé from the Loire Valley in North Eastern France. You may pay more for these wines, but they deliver on depth and mineral notes that add a few extra layers to Sauvignon Blanc. Loire Sauvignon Blanc can also display less fruit forward notes but it's a region that varies from year to year, so if you hit on a warm vintage, you will see them swing more towards tropical fruits while still being refreshing.

Pro Tip: *Serve Sauvignon Blanc in a slimmer wine glass to appreciate the aromatics of this grape!*

PULLED JACKFRUIT MINI SUBS

Serves 4-6

This is a fun backyard meal. It is truly amazing how much the texture of jackfruit mimics that of pulled pork. A lot of similar recipes online call for the jackfruit to be cooked on the stove and then transferred to the oven. The entire process takes a couple of hours and quite frankly, who has the time? I've skipped the oven altogether and found that the result doesn't skimp on taste at all.

SLAW

2 cups cabbage, shredded (green and/ or purple)

1/2 cup carrot, julienned

1/4 cup vegan mayo

1 tbsp lemon juice

1 tbsp apple cider vinegar

1/2 tsp agave or white sugar

Salt & pepper

PULLED JACKFRUIT

1 can of unripe jackfruit in water or brine

1 tbsp olive oil

1 small onion, diced

2 cloves garlic, minced

1 tbsp Cajun spice mix

1/2 tsp smoked paprika

1 tsp cumin

1/2 tsp liquid smoke

1 cup vegetable broth

2 tbsp dry white wine

1/2 cup vegan BBQ sauce of choice

MAKE THE SLAW

Whisk all ingredients in a bowl until well blended. Toss cabbage with the dressing and refrigerate for at least an hour.

MAKE THE PULLED JACKFRUIT

To prepare the jackfruit, first drain the can. The pieces come as little triangles. If the core is very tough, remove it. Otherwise, finely chop it and then pull apart the remaining fruit with 2 forks until it resembles pulled pork.

Sauté onion in a frying pan over medium heat for 2 minutes. Add garlic and sauté for another couple of minutes until soft. Add jackfruit and toss to mix well.

Meanwhile, In a small bowl whisk together spices, liquid smoke, broth, wine and BBQ sauce. Add spice mixture to the pan. Simmer, lightly covered, for 30 minutes stirring occasionally until the sauce is thick and glazed.

Serve on hamburger buns or mini submarine rolls with coleslaw.

Optional serving suggestion: Turn these into jackfruit tacos with soft, corn tortillas instead!

Admittedly this is my favourite summer alternative to serve at a BBQ because this dish is great with some chips or French fries, keeping it nice and casual.

With that, my value pick is an Ontario Gamay Noir from Niagara, Canada. Bright red fruits and slight pepper notes with soft tannins work so well with the sweet spiciness of the sauce in the jackfruit, yet it doesn't overpower it. It's a fun alternative to Beaujolais but if it's too hard to find where you are, go for the Beaujolais.

For my splurge wine I am going in a totally different direction with a Rosé Champagne from Champagne, France. First off, I love the cheekiness of serving an expensive Champagne with barbeque! That said, the Rosé bubbles work so well with this meal. The red fruit in the wine matches with the sweetness in the sauce and the bubbles also work so well with anything deep fried so that side of chips or fries will also be happy with this match! Small Grower Champagnes can be a fun alternative to the big names you usually find.

Pro Tip: *If you don't want to spend the dollars on a Champagne, find a good Traditional Method Sparkling Rosé from anywhere in the world and it will work just as well.*

RESTAURANT-WORTHY RED CURRY

Serves 4

Spicy Asian food is notoriously difficult to pair with wine, but Jen has some great choices for this meal! In my humble opinion, this curry is close to restaurant-quality. It is a bit involved because you're elevating a jarred curry paste by adding fresh ingredients to it.

Note: *Vegetables will be added at different times depending on how long they each take to cook, making this a recipe where 'mise en place' or 'everything in its place' is a good practice. Keep each vegetable in it's own bowl for ease of dropping into the pot when called for.*

PASTE

1 tbsp each ginger and garlic, minced

1-2 small Thai red chillies, seeded

2-3 fresh kaffir lime leaves (or one dried, which you'll add later)

1 roasted red pepper (jarred)

1 tbsp tomato paste

1 tbsp vegan red curry paste

1 stalk lemongrass, the top 2 - 3 inches of the white parts minced (stalk should be heavy, if they're too light they are likely dried out and will be too tough to be palatable)

1/4 cup chopped cilantro, stems and leaves

2 tbsp low sodium soy or tamari sauce

1 tbsp sesame oil

CURRY

1 tbsp coconut oil

1 can coconut milk

1/2 cup water or vegetable broth

3 cups mixed vegetables, cut into larger than bite-size pieces (any combination of mushrooms, sweet peppers, broccoli, potatoes, sweet potatoes, carrots, snap peas, cauliflower, bok choy)

1 cup firm tofu, lightly browned in coconut oil, before cutting into bite-sized pieces

Steamed brown or jasmine rice

Garnish - chopped cilantro, crushed peanuts, lime wedges

MAKE THE PASTE

Mix ginger, garlic, chillies, kaffir leaves, red pepper, tomato paste, curry paste, lemongrass, soy sauce and sesame oil a mini-chopper or food processor and blend until smooth, scraping down sides as needed.

MAKE THE CURRY

Heat oil in a large pot over medium heat. Add curry paste from the blender and cook for one minute until fragrant. Add coconut milk, water/broth and firm vegetables (potatoes, carrots, sweet potatoes). Cook covered until the contents are boiling.

Next, add dried kaffir lime leaf (if using), reduce heat to medium low and cook for another 5-7 minutes.

Add the softer veggies (mushrooms, sweet peppers, bok choy, snap peas, etc.) along with the tofu and cook until vegetables are fork-tender but not mushy, about 4-5 minutes, adding broccoli and cauliflower in the final couple of minutes.

Serve in bowls, with steamed rice and lime wedges on the side. Top with cilantro and peanuts.

For my value pick I am going in a very different direction than wine, straight to a Singha beer. These beers are produced in Thailand and considered the original Thai beer. The flavours are full bodied and rich, with balanced hopes and are golden yellow in colour. Depending on how spicy and hot you go with your curry, it's important to note that higher alcohol can drive up the spice on your palate so the 5% alcohol on this beer keeps the heat in check.

For my splurge I am not really splurging, but instead suggested an interesting alternative, a low alcohol wine. The world is creating some excellent intentional low alcohol wines now and I particularly like some examples I have tried from the Sauvignon Blanc grape made in Marlborough, New Zealand. I find you don't really miss any of the flavour of Sauvignon Blanc, however the low alcohol works great with the heat of this dish. The green notes in the Sauvignon Blanc work perfectly with the cilantro, peas and broccoli in the dish. It's a really fun alternative!

IMAM BAYILDI (TURKISH EGGPLANT)

Serves 4-6

This is a Turkish dish that I fell hard for when I visited Istanbul. Boy oh boy, the things the Turks do with vegetables! The dried currants are the magic ingredient here as they add a depth of sweetness to a vegetable that is usually served in a very savoury manner. Add some crusty bread and a green salad with a lemon vinaigrette and you've got a lovely summer meal.

2 large Italian eggplants sliced in half lengthwise, stems attached

1/4 cup olive oil + 1 tsp

1 cup tomatoes, chopped

1/2 cup red onion, diced

1/4 cup fresh mint, chopped

3 medium cloves garlic, minced

2 tbsp good quality balsamic vinegar

2 tbsp currants

1/4 cup pine nuts

Salt & pepper

Preheat oven to 350 °F.

Cut 2-3 slits into eggplant lengthwise. Brush with 1/4 tsp olive oil and fry cut side down for 5-6 minutes. Place cut side up in roasting pan.

In medium bowl mix chopped tomatoes, red onion, mint, garlic, balsamic, 1/4 cup olive oil, currants and pine nuts. Season with salt & pepper. Taste and add more balsamic if needed as mixture should be slightly sweet. Divide mixture between eggplants, pressing into the cuts.

Bake in oven for 30-40 minutes until fork tender.

My value pick is a red wine made with the Malbec grape in Argentina. This grape was brought from settlers who arrived in Argentina from France, where it historically helped make up the red Bordeaux blend of grapes. It is now a signature red wine of Argentina and with good reason. Transplanted here, it can be rich, warm, spicy and have some tannin and distinct blueberry notes that play well off the warmth in this dish. Look for a Malbec from the Mendoza region.

My splurge wine is a Syrah from Paso Robles in Southern California, USA. These wines can be rich, full-bodied and so decadent but also just the right wine you'd want to have on a cold evening with this comforting dish. Known in most of the new world wine regions as Shiraz, decadent Syrah from Paso Robles reaches its full, rich and wonderful potential. This is definitely a full-bodied style of wine.

Pro Tip: *Don't be afraid to decant these wines and be sure to serve in a larger Bordeaux style wine glass.*

FALL HARVEST MOUSSAKA

Serves 6-8

Moussaka could be considered a Greek-style lasagna topped with bechamel sauce, which is traditionally made with flour and milk. Lo and behold, pine nuts blended with tofu make an excellent vegan bechamel. This is for those elegant dinner parties, holiday gatherings or simply when you want a meal that's truly special because it takes a bit more love and patience. While it has several steps, it's not difficult, just time-consuming.

VEGETABLE LAYER

1 large, Italian eggplant

2-3 large zucchini

3 large potatoes

Olive oil for brushing

Salt

SAUCE

1 tbsp olive oil

1 large onion or 4 medium shallots, diced

4-6 cloves garlic, thinly sliced

1/3 cup full bodied red wine

1 cup vegetarian ground 'beef', cooked lentils, or a combination

1 x 24 oz can crushed tomatoes

1/2 tsp cinnamon

2 tsp oregano

1 bay leaf

1 tsp packed brown sugar

1/2 tsp salt

Black pepper to taste

PINE NUT BECHAMEL

1/2 cup pine nuts or raw cashews (if using cashew, soak in water for at least 10 minutes before using)

3 tbsp lemon juice

1 generous cup soft or medium tofu

1 large clove garlic, minced

1/2 tsp ground nutmeg

1-1 1/2 tsp salt

MAKE THE VEGETABLES

Preheat the oven to 400 °F.

Cut the tops and ends off the eggplant and zucchini. Slice all vegetables horizontally into ½ inch pieces. Place the vegetables on lightly greased baking sheets. Brush with oil on the sides facing up. Sprinkle eggplant and zucchini lightly with salt. Broil for 12-14 slightly tender but not fully cooked as they will continue to cook during main baking time.

Meanwhile, prepare the tomato sauce.

MAKE THE SAUCES

In a medium pot cook the onions in oil over medium heat for 2-3 minutes. Add garlic and cook for another minute. Add wine and ground 'beef' and/or lentils, and simmer until wine has absorbed. Add tomatoes, spices and sugar. Simmer for 15-20 minutes.

While the sauce is simmering, prepare the bechamel layer.

MAKE THE PINE NUT BECHAMEL

In a blender combine pine nuts with lemon juice for about 30 seconds at high speed. Scrape down as needed. Add rest of ingredients and blend until a smooth, creamy sauce forms, about 1 1/2-2 minutes.

ASSEMBLY

Preheat the oven to 350 °F.

Remove bay leaf and place a thin layer of sauce on the bottom of a 9x13 casserole dish. Layer potatoes onto the sauce, and cover with half of the remaining sauce. Add zucchini followed by the eggplant and top with the rest of the sauce. Pour bechamel on top and spread evenly with a spoon.

Bake for 25-30 minutes until the top is lightly browned. The finished dish should rest for 10-15 minutes to let it firm up. It firms up even better if reheated and served the next day.

Serve with crusty bread and, of course, a Greek salad!

This is a warm, rich and spice laden dish that reminds me of crisp autumn days and warmth from the fireplace, when I just want to curl up with a warm blanket, a glass of red and Priya's Moussaka.

My value pick wine for this heartwarming dish is a Carménère from Chile. These wines are based on the Carménère grape which was one of the original red grapes allowed in Bordeaux (they can be part of a Bordeaux blend). It's rich without being overly decadent, slightly spicy, and it often has intriguing roasted red pepper notes. This is the ideal wine for this dish as all the spices and roasted notes play off each other in perfect harmony.

For my splurge wine I would go to Australia and select a Shiraz from the Barossa Valley. You can definitely find some with a value price point, but I find when you spend a little more money on Barossa Valley Shiraz, the quality goes up exponentially. Shiraz is naturally spicy (think black peppercorns) and can often have uplifting eucalyptus notes from this region specifically. Again, this is a rich style of red, which can be tricky to pair with vegan food but this dish is so flavourful and rich itself, that the pairing actually works.

Pro Tip: *While it may seem counter-intuitive, I suggest you serve both of these reds slightly chilled, otherwise the alcohol will seem bigger and clash with the spices of the dish rather than meld with them.*

MEDITERRANEAN STUFFED PEPPERS WITH WHITE WINE DRIZZLE

Serves 4

This dish has a bit of a retro feel to me, it's classic yet timeless. I've opted to replace the traditional rice with couscous for slightly lower calories. It's such a comforting meal but the presentation makes it feel upscale and the wine drizzle takes it up a notch from being just-another-stuffed-pepper recipe.

PEPPERS

4 bell peppers (I use a combo of red, yellow and red)

1 tbsp oil

1 small onion, roughly chopped

1 medium zucchini, diced

1 cup cherry tomatoes, quartered

2 small cloves garlic, roughly chopped

1/4 cup dry white wine

1/2 tsp salt

Black pepper to taste

1 1/2 cups cooked couscous (see cooking instructions in note below)

1/4 cup sundried tomatoes, chopped (drain, if using jarred)

WHITE WINE DRIZZLE

2 large tomatoes, finely diced

1 tbsp fresh garlic, minced

2 tbsp dry white wine

1/4 tsp salt and a few grinds of black pepper

MAKE THE PEPPERS

Preheat the oven to 350 °F.

Slice the tops off the bell peppers and remove with stem in place. Remove membranes and slice a small piece off the bottoms if needed to make sure they stand up straight in a dish.

Pre-bake the bell peppers for 8-10 minutes.

In the meantime, heat oil in a large frying pan over medium heat and cook onion and zucchini for 3-5 minutes. Add cherry tomatoes and garlic and cook for another 2 minutes. Add wine and cook for 5-7 minutes until zucchini is tender but not mushy.

Separate the cooked couscous with a fork, and add it along with the sundried tomatoes to the vegetable blend and mix well. Season with extra salt & pepper if needed.

Pack the peppers with stuffing, cover with 'tops' and bake for 15 minutes.

MAKE THE WHITE WINE DRIZZLE

While the peppers are baking, bring all ingredients to a boil in a small pot. Reduce heat and simmer for 8-10 minutes until it reaches the consistency of a thin sauce. Puree and set aside until ready to use.

Serve alongside peppers to allow guests to drizzle as much, or little, as they like.

Note: *How to Cook Couscous (Makes 2 1/2 cups)*

1 cup vegetable broth
1 tbsp olive oil
1 cup couscous

Bring broth to a boil in a small pot.

Remove the pan from heat, add olive oil and the couscous and stir to blend evenly. Cover and set aside for 5-7 minutes until all moisture is absorbed. Fluff with a fork before using.

Always in style, always delicious and a favourite for both, kids and adults in the family, this is also an easy dish to really dress up with wine.

My value pick for this is a Pinot Gris from Oregon, USA. While we may know this grape as Pinot Grigio thanks to the big Italian brands making it a marketing success, it is grown in a few places in the world and does quite well in the hills of Northern Oregon. Pinot Gris/Grigio is fresh and light, if not somewhat neutral at times, but makes an excellent companion to food. The natural bitterness in the wine will complement the green notes of the peppers in this dish.

For my splurge wine I am sticking to the same grape variety but traveling to Northern France to the charming wine region of Alsace. The Pinot Gris here has more weight, texture and a fuller mouth feel. It also has more fruit aromas of peaches and honey. The weight of this wine works well with the density of the couscous, but it still has enough acidity to clean your palate.

Pro Tip: *Good Alsatian Pinot Gris (like Grand Cru) can age well in your cellar and really improve, even over decades. Use some of your selected wine for the white wine sauce.*

GREEN SOBA SALAD

Serves 4

When it's hot outside, the last place I want to be is beside a hot stove. I'd much rather soak up the natural heat! This satisfying salad packs a nutritional punch and takes no time to put together. It's fresh, filling and looks impressive while being a snap to throw together-what more could you ask for on a summer's day?

1 x 227 g package soba noodles (use brown rice soba for a gluten free dish)

2 tbsp soy sauce

1 tbsp maple syrup

1 tbsp rice wine vinegar

1 tbsp ginger, grated

1 tbsp white miso paste

2 tbsp orange juice

1 tbsp sesame oil

1/2 of a 420 g package firm tofu, cut into 1/2 inch cubes

1 cup snap peas, ends trimmed

1/2 cup edamame (if using frozen, let thaw to room temperature)

1/4 cup green onions, sliced

Chopped coriander for garnish

Cook soba in boiling water for 7-9 minutes. Be careful not to overcook. Drain and set aside.

Combine soy sauce, maple syrup, rice wine vinegar, ginger, miso paste, orange juice and sesame oil in a large bowl. Add noodles, snap peas, tofu, edamame and green onions and toss to coat well.

Serve with coriander on top or on the side.

I love the chilled Soba here and this dish is all about fresh, green flavours. Snap peas, green onions and cilantro dominate so it's green and crunchy. The principle of colour matching here works well when it comes to wine.

My value pick, Vinho Verde (translation Green Wine), from Northern Portugal is an awesome match. These wines are lower in alcohol, tart and fresh with a slight spritz. The greenish quality of the wine works well with all the green notes in the dish, yet it doesn't overpower it.

My splurge wine would be a high end Grüner Veltliner from Kamptal or Wachau, Austria. These wines often display notes of lentil and fennel and generally are green and crunchy. These whites are deceptive because while they have vibrant acidity, they can have amazing weight and texture along with a long finish, especially when you spend a bit more on them.

Pro Tip: *Wines with green notes themselves tend to work well with green food. Have fun here 'colour matching'.*

VIETNAMESE LAYERED NOODLE SALAD

Serves 4-6

I'm not one for salads as a main course but throw in some rice noodles, tofu and chopped peanuts and I'm on board. I am obsessed with this dish and eat it at least once a week in the hotter months. The crunch of the peanuts and the crispiness of the lettuce are just so satisfying while the tofu helps give it the heartiness that my bottomless-pit of a stomach requires. Can be served chilled or at room temperature.

TOFU

1/2 of a 420 g package tofu, cut into 1/2 inch thick slices

Juice of one lime

3 tbsp soy sauce or Tamari

2 tbsp agave

1 tbsp white miso paste

1 tbsp rice wine vinegar

1 tsp ginger, minced

1 large clove garlic minced

SAUCE

3 cloves garlic, minced

1 small Thai red chili, minced

2 tbsp agave

1 cup hot water

2 small limes, juiced

2 tbsp soy sauce

NOODLES & TOPPINGS

1/2 a 400 g package rice vermicelli

2 cups romaine lettuce, roughly chopped

1 cup cucumber, thinly sliced

1 cup julienned carrots

Garnish with chopped fresh mint, and crushed peanuts

MAKE THE TOFU

Prick the tofu with a fork on both sides to let the marinade soak through. Combine all ingredients and pour over tofu in a shallow dish. Let marinate for at least an hour, flipping at least once.

In a large frying pan, the tofu at medium-high heat in its marinade for 3-5 minutes on each side until golden. The marinade will thicken and add a sort of a flavoured skin to the tofu. Remove from heat and cut into bite-size pieces.

MAKE THE SAUCE

In the meantime, mix garlic and chilis together. In a small bowl combine the agave and boiled water. Add the lime juice, soy sauce and chili garlic blend. Set aside.

NOODLES AND ASSEMBLY

Soak noodles according to package instructions in boiling water for 5-6 minutes until soft. Drain and rinse quickly under cold water before tossing with tofu and sauce. Top with veggies, crushed peanuts, mint and a wedge of lime or serve all toppings on the side and let guests layer their own bowls.

This is a crunchy, refreshing, summery dish with a bit of a kick!

My value pick is a wine and grape you may have never had nor heard of. I am going with the white Semillon grape where it has long made a name for itself in the Hunter Valley region of Australia. This grape, transported from Bordeaux in France, produces an almost water-white, citrusy, dry wine with notes of lanolin, straw, grass and subtle green herbs in this particular climate. These wines have high acidity and lower alcohol which makes them a perfect partner to the nuts and marinated tofu.

My splurge wine is going further south in Australia to the island of Tasmania. Here, I recommend a Pinot Noir which thrives in the cool climate of the Tamar Valley and produces a tiny but precious amount of unique and terroir-driven reds. These wines are all about finesse and elegance with really bright fruit that stand up to this flavourful dish. In addition, the wines do not have too much alcohol or tannins to battle with the heat, making it a match made in heaven.

Pro Tip: *Hunter Valley Semillon ages extremely well. If you can buy a bit extra and tuck it away for five to ten years, you will see it turn into a marvel.*

SPICY SATAY-STYLE NOODLES

Serves 6

There's something about a peanut sauce that screams 'comfort food' to me and this dish is the perfect example. It's an 'everything-in-the-kitchen-sink' type of dish as it has so many veggies. I like my food on the spicy side, but you can downplay the amount of chilli garlic sauce according to your palate.

1/2 of a 400 g package flat rice noodles

1 cup small broccoli florets

1/2 cup unsalted vegetable broth

1 cup coconut milk

3 to 5 tbsp soy sauce

2-3 tbsp maple syrup or agave

1/2 cup creamy peanut butter (preferably unsweetened)

2-2 1/2 tbsp chilli garlic sauce

1 tsp ginger, grated

2-3 cloves garlic, minced

1 tbsp sesame oil

1/2-1 cup shredded carrots

2-3 green onions, thinly sliced into 1 inch strips

1 cup extra firm tofu, cut into 1/2 inch cubes and well browned in sesame oil

1 small, yellow or orange bell pepper, thinly sliced

Garnish: Crushed peanuts, chopped cilantro and lime wedges

In a large pot, boil 2-3 inches of water. Add noodles and cook according to package instructions.

Remove from heat and add broccoli, keeping the pot slightly uncovered so broccoli can steam-cook for 2-3 minutes. Drain and set aside.

In a medium pot over medium low heat, whisk vegetable broth, coconut milk, tamari/soy sauce, maple syrup/agave, peanut butter, chilli garlic sauce, fresh ginger and garlic until it comes to a light boil. Reduce heat and simmer for 3-5 minutes. Remove from heat and add sesame oil so peanut butter doesn't separate and get lumpy.

In a large pot, combine noodles with sauce. Toss in broccoli, carrots, green onions, tofu, and bell pepper until well-blended. Top with crushed peanuts and cilantro. Serve with lime wedges.

While I like this dish warm, it also works when served chilled.

For my value pick I am recommending an off-dry Riesling from Ontario, Canada. Ontario has a cold winter and long fall which is perfect for developing this grape and ripening it while maintaining the acidity. The hint of sweetness in the wine will help balance the spice in the dish but works well with tricky cilantro and bell pepper.

For my splurge wine I am going with a Chenin Blanc from the Loire Valley in France. Look for a Vouvray-Demi Sec that, again, has some residual sweetness to it. These wines are glorious on their own but can be surprising matches with food, especially with nut-based cheese and any dish with spice. They offer a range of price points too, from very top-quality Vouvray to simple and pleasant expressions.

Pro Tip: *Reminder, don't pair a high alcohol wine with a spicy dish. It will make the wine taste more alcoholic than it is. And if all else fails, beer works great!*

CURRANT & MINT CABBAGE ROLLS

Serves 8

You know which dried herb is not used often enough? Mint. I got it into my head one day that I wanted to make cabbage rolls but with a minty twist. Not sure why this got stuck in my brain but I'm glad it did because it inspired this "Mediterranean-esque" recipe. I threw in dried currants to really switch up a traditionally Polish dish. They add a lovely hint of sweetness and turn a rustic comfort food into an elegant dish you can proudly serve at a winter dinner party. Make it extra pretty by using a combination of green and red cabbage leaves!

SAUCE

1 x 680 ml can tomato sauce (reserving 1/2 cup for rolls)

1 tsp balsamic vinegar

2 tsp maple syrup

1 tsp dried mint

CABBAGE ROLLS

1 head green cabbage, cored

1 1/2 tsp salt, plus more for the water

1 tbsp olive oil

1/2 cup onion, finely chopped

1 medium zucchini, shredded

1 cup cooked rice

1 1/2 cups vegan ground 'beef'

1 1/2 tbsp full-bodied red wine

2 tsp dried mint

2 tbsp dried currants

1/4 cup canned tomato sauce

Lightly brush a 9x13 inch casserole dish with olive oil.

Heat sauce ingredients over medium heat in a medium pot until they reach a light simmer. Cook for 3-5 minutes and remove from the stove.

Gently peel off the first 8-10 leaves from the cabbage and cut out the hard stem part. Bring a large pot with 2 inches of water to a boil. Add cabbage leaves and steam for 3-5 minutes until wilted and easy to manipulate. Remove from heat, drain and let cool while you prepare the stuffing.

In a large frying pan over medium heat onion 2-3 mins. Add zucchini and cook until liquid is absorbed. Add rice, ground 'beef' and wine. Let the wine absorb. Add mint and currants, then season with minimal salt and pepper. Add the 1/2 cup of sauce and combine well.

Preheat the oven to 350 °F.

Pour half a cup of sauce to cover the bottom of the casserole dish.

Take a leaf and place it curved side down on a cutting board. Place a quarter cup of filling into the center, fold in the sides and then roll up. Place seam side down into the casserole dish. Repeat until all the filling is used up.

Pour remaining sauce on top and bake, uncovered for 25 minutes.

Cover and bake for an additional 10 minutes.

This is an earthy and spicy version of the classic with a very flavorful tomato sauce. Dried mint and currants add amazing Mediterranean vibes to this dish.

My value pick is a red wine from Greece, made from the Agiorgitiko which is widely grown in the Nemea region of Peloponnese but can now be found throughout Greece. This grape produces wines which typically have plum notes, some spice and a lovely earthiness, which really work in harmony with the tomatoes and spices in this dish.

My splurge wine would be a very good Valpolicella Ripasso from Veneto, Italy. This red wine can be a blend of red grapes and when made in the 'Ripasso' method, can change it from a simple to a more robust wine. The production method of a Ripasso means the wine is created with partially dried grape skins that have been left over from Amarone or Recioto wines. These reds work with the tomato sauce so well and stand up to all the exotic spices in this dish effortlessly with that extra degree of fruitiness imparted by the winemaking.

Pro Tip: *When selecting your Valpolicella Ripasso, read the label carefully. There are many styles of Valpolicella such as Recioto, Amarone and simple Valpolicella.*

STUFFED SPAGHETTI SQUASH 'PASTA'

Serves 4

I absolutely love pasta but in the dog days of summer, even I want something a bit lighter. Enter the aptly-named 'spaghetti' squash! It's like Mother Nature anticipated our needs and provided for us. The olives give this a Mediterranean spin and makes me think of lazy days basking under the sun amongst the blue-domed buildings in Santorini. Ahh memories!

1 spaghetti squash
Salt and pepper
2 tbsp olive oil
1 small red onion, diced
3 cloves garlic, roughly chopped
1/4 cup dry white wine
1 heaping cup tomatoes, diced
2 tbsp Kalamata olives, chopped
Salt & pepper
Vegan parmesan

Preheat the oven to 400 °F.

Cut squash in half lengthwise. Brush the cut sides with olive oil and sprinkle with salt and pepper. Place on a lightly greased baking dish, cut side up, and roast for 30-40 minutes until soft.

Once the squash is roasted, use a fork to pull out the 'spaghetti' fine strings.

While squash is roasting, sauté onions for 2-3 minutes. Add garlic and sauté for another couple of minutes. Add the wine and tomatoes, cooking until most of the wine is absorbed, about 5-7 minutes. Add olives before adjusting seasoning with salt and pepper, as the olives may already be quite salty.

Toss 'spaghetti' with vegetables. Serve inside the squash 'shells' or in bowls with vegan parmesan on top.

Note: *Olives fresh from the deli counter will be saltier than jarred olives so the amount of salt needed will vary.*

For all of us wanting or needing gluten-free options, this dish is amazing. It's light and summery and could even be served as a side dish.

My value pick is similarly a fun and light Moscofilero from Mantinea, Greece. This is a lovely dry white wine with aromatic flavours of peach, nectarine and apricot along with a delicate nuttiness. This pasta dish has tomatoes and olives, and this pretty wine plays off these challenges and easily cleanses your palate from any residual richness.

For my splurge pick I am going to a beautiful Canadian wine from British Columbia and recommending a red alternative, Pinot Noir. These wines are at their best from the Okanagan Valley. They are super bright, fruity, and loaded with beautiful, tart berry flavours and mouth-watering acidity. The very elegant Pinot does well in the cooler pockets of this region like Kelowna and it shows off this tomato-based pasta dish so well.

Pro Tip: *Serve both white and red recommendations cool, but not cold.*

POWERED-UP PESTO PASTA SALAD

Serves 4

This is a great way to use up all that basil in your garden! I've powered up this recipe with fresh veggies and chickpeas for added protein, nutrients and colour. I add parsley for an extra zing of brightness. If actual garlic is too strong for you, try garlic scapes instead, just be sure to omit the bulb.

1/2 of a 375 g package fusilli

1 cup packed fresh basil leaves

1/4 cup packed fresh flat-leaf parsley leaves

3-4 tbsp fresh lemon juice

2 medium cloves garlic (or 6-8 garlic scapes), roughly chopped

1/2 - 1 tsp salt

1/3 cup olive oil

3-4 tbsp nutritional yeast

1/2 cup walnuts

2-3 tbsp water, if needed

1 pint cherry tomatoes, halved or quartered

1 x 15 oz can chickpeas, rinsed and drained

1/2 cup cucumber, diced

1/2 cup red or yellow bell pepper, diced

Salt and freshly grated black pepper

Bring a large pot of heavily salted water to boil for the pasta. Cook the pasta until al dente, about 7 minutes or according to package instructions. Set aside.

Meanwhile, prepare the pesto by adding all ingredients to a food processor or blender. Add lemon, salt and nutritional yeast in increments as it's easier to add flavour than it is to remove it. Blend until smooth, stopping frequently to scrape down the sides and adding water if the mixture is too thick.

Toss pasta with half of the pesto, chickpeas and chopped veggies. Add more pesto as needed if the pasta seems too dry, and more salt & lemon for final touches.

Note: *Try slices of fresh apple to get rid of that garlic breath. The enzyme that turns apples brown if they sit out too long also acts as a natural deodorant to the bad-breath causing sulphides in garlic.*

I love this salad - either cold or warm, as a side dish or a main course. Consider using chickpea pasta as an alternative, just be careful not to overcook!

My value pick is a wine hailing from Austria, and not grown much outside of the country. Grüner Veltliner is a great match with this dish. Grüner naturally has lots of green notes (like chives, radish and lentils) along with vibrant acidity. It actually works with many green foods in general which can sometimes be tricky to match wine with. Try one from the region of Kamptal.

My splurge wine recommendation would be a Chianti Classico Reserva from Tuscany, Italy. This wine is based on the Sangiovese grape and has cherry, tomato and tomato leaf notes that make it earthy with a fresh finish. Not just for pizza, these wines work well with tomatoes, olives and basil (what grows together, goes together).

Pro Tip: *Be sure to decant the Chianti a few hours ahead of time if it's a newer vintage so it can breathe.*

PASTA ALFREDO-ISH

Serves 4

Dairy is often the one food group that many have the hardest time giving up as they make the transition to a plant-based lifestyle. I was never a milk drinker but having to give up cheese on pizza and pasta may have caused a few tantrums reminiscent of a toddler. The secret in this alfredo-esque cream sauce is raw cashews, while the sundried tomatoes add a burst of flavour to balance out the creamy weight of the sauce.

1/2 of a 375 g package of rotini

1 cup broccoli, chopped into small florets

1 large onion, chopped

4-6 cloves garlic, minced

1 cup raw cashews, soaked in water for 10 minutes, then drained

1 1/2 cups vegetable broth

2 tbsp olive oil

1 - 1 1/2 tbsp lemon juice

1 - 2 tsp sea salt

1 tbsp nutritional yeast

1/4 - 1/2 tsp freshly ground black pepper

1/4 cup sundried tomatoes, julienned or diced (if using jarred, make sure they're well-drained)

Boil pasta according to package directions, remembering to heavily salt your water. Add broccoli during the last minute of cooking and leave uncovered, to prevent the broccoli from browning. Drain and set aside.

In a medium pot and over medium heat, cook onion in 1 tablespoon olive oil for 2-3 minutes. Add garlic and cook until soft. Place into a blender along with cashews, vegetable broth, remaining 1 tablespoon olive oil, lemon juice, sea salt and nutritional yeast and blend on high until smooth, about 2 minutes or so. Taste and add additional salt and pepper if needed.

Toss hot pasta and broccoli with cream sauce and sundried tomatoes. Serve immediately.

This dish instantly transports me to Tuscany and makes me reminisce to days spent sitting under the Tuscan sun while eating a bowl of delicious pasta.

A delicate and zesty white wine from Tuscany would be amazing with this dish, and Trebbiano is grown all over The region. This crisp white has loads of citrus fruit which will play off the lemon notes in the dish. There's also a bit of a bitter finish, echoing the broccoli, while the acidity cuts through those cashews, leaving you wanting the next bite. Amoré!

For my splurge wine match, I am recommending a white wine from France's Northern Rhône Valley region, made from the grapes Marsanne and Roussanne. These are truly special wines that have dense weight and texture to them, a very creamy body (echoing this dish), a distinct nuttiness to flirt with the cashews and a zippy citrus finish. These are complex wines! Look for Hermitage Blanc and don't be afraid to age it for 5-10 years to see it sing. If you can't find this rare white, you can substitute with a white Crozes-Hermitage.

Pro Tip: *Serve the Trebbiano well chilled but for the Hermitage Blanc, I would serve this at or about 12 °C, so you're able to appreciate the beautiful nuances of this stellar wine. Don't be afraid to decant the Hermitage Blanc, it could use an hour or two of air before serving.*

CHEESY PENNE FOR GROWN-UPS

Serves 6

Who doesn't love a bowl of creamy, cheesy pasta? Here's a great version that can be made gluten free by using rice pasta and gluten-free flour. When I'm serving this at a dinner party, I use penne rather than macaroni, because it feels a bit more elegant, that's why I call this a recipe for 'grown-ups'!

1/2 of a 375 g package of penne or macaroni

1 tsp salt for pasta water

1/2 cup broccoli, cut into small florets

1 tbsp olive oil

1 small onion, chopped

3 cloves garlic, chopped

1 small white potato, diced

1/4 cup carrot, chopped

1 1/2 cups raw cashews

2 tbsp tomato paste

1 tbsp garlic powder

1 cup vegetable broth

1/2 cup nutritional yeast

1/2 cup unsweetened almond milk

1-2 tbsp lemon juice

1/2 tsp yellow mustard

1 tsp salt

Black pepper

Bring a large pot of salted water to a boil. Cook pasta according to package directions, adding broccoli during the last minute of cooking. Drain and set aside.

In a medium pot, cook onions, garlic, potato and carrots in oil for 3-5 minutes. Add cashews, tomato paste, garlic powder and vegetable broth, simmering until potatoes are soft.

Pour into a blender, along with nutritional yeast, almond milk, lemon juice, mustard and salt and blend until smooth, about 2-3 minutes. Season with salt and pepper. Pour over pasta and stir to combine. Serve immediately.

Note: *the less pasta you use, the more creamy and cheesy the end result will be so if you prefer a drier version, simply cook more pasta.*

Matching this with a wine makes a homey meal complete and really helps to elevate it!

My value pick is a wine that contrasts the dish. I'm recommending a white Rueda from Spain. These wines are a blend of Sauvignon Blanc among a few other grapes and it provides a refreshing contrast to the creaminess in this dish. These are some of the most loved and best-selling white wines in Spain and they come in a variety of styles and price points, so be as adventurous as you like.

My splurge goes in the opposite direction with a delicious Chardonnay from Willamette Valley in Oregon, USA. These creamy, rich and sometimes buttery wines are a perfect complement to Mac & Cheese, really echoing its texture beautifully. More decadent and rich than the value pick, they also have a lovely mineral lift to them and I would serve this on a cold evening as it's a great alternative to a weighty red wine.

Pro Tip: *Chardonnay grows well all over the world but especially in moderate to cooler climates so feel free to explore!*

NONNA'S NEW WORLD LASAGNA

Serves 6-8

If I could only choose one cuisine (other than Indian food of course) to eat for the rest of my life it would be Italian food, and lasagna is one of my favourite meals. This recipe has many steps because of all the layers. It's a labour of love and one that is well worth the time. I like to think of Nonna spending a Sunday afternoon preparing this for supper with the grandkids. It fills me with a sense of family and laughter!

SAUCE

1/4 cup olive oil

1 large onion, chopped

8 cloves garlic, chopped

1/4 cup full bodied red wine

2 tbsp tomato paste

2 cans diced tomato

3/4 tsp salt (slightly more if using unsalted canned tomatoes)

10-12 turns of the pepper mill

1 tsp dried basil

2 cups vegan ground 'beef'

VEGETABLE LAYER

2 tbsp olive oil

2 large Portobello mushrooms, cut in 1/2" slices

1 large zucchini, sliced in 1/2" rounds

1 small red onion, chopped

4 cloves garlic, roughly chopped

1/2 tsp salt

Black pepper

1/4 cup full-bodied red wine

1 bunch baby spinach

TOFU RICOTTA

1/2 cup raw cashews soaked in water for 10 mins, then drained

1 x 420 g block medium tofu

2 tbsp fresh lemon juice

1/4 cup vegetable broth

3 tbsp nutritional yeast

3 cloves garlic

1/2 cup packed fresh basil, chopped

1 tsp salt

Black pepper

1 x 375 g package oven-ready lasagna noodles

Shredded Vegan Mozzarella (optional)

Parmesan (optional)

MAKE THE SAUCE

Sauté onion in oil for 2-3 minutes over medium-high heat. Add garlic and sauté until softened. Add red wine and cook until absorbed. Add tomato paste and sauté just until blended. Add tomatoes, salt and pepper and bring to a boil. Reduce heat to low, cover and simmer for 3 hours stirring occasionally. Remove from heat and use a hand blender to puree the sauce. Set aside 1/2 cup for layering on the bottom of the baking pan.

Place back on the stove, add basil and vegan ground beef, and simmer for another 10 minutes. Remove from the stove, taste and adjust salt and pepper if needed and let cool while you prepare the vegetables and tofu ricotta.

MAKE THE VEGETABLE LAYER

Sauté onion and garlic in oil for 2-3 minutes in a large frying pan over medium heat. Add mushrooms, zucchini, salt and a few grinds of pepper. Cook until liquid from mushrooms is absorbed, about 7-10 minutes. Add red wine and cook until wine is absorbed. Add spinach, cover and cook another minute or so, just until wilted and remove from heat. Adjust seasoning with salt and pepper if needed.

MAKE THE TOFU RICOTTA

Drain cashews and tofu. Add all ingredients to a blender and blend until smooth, about 60-90 seconds.

ASSEMBLY

Preheat the oven to 375 °F.

Spread half a cup of sauce on the bottom of a 9x13 pan and add a layer of oven-ready lasagna noodles. Coat with a cup of sauce. Add vegetable mixture and cover with another layer of noodles. Cover with tofu ricotta. Add another layer of noodles and pour 2 cups of sauce on top. Finish with vegan mozzarella if using, cover with aluminum foil and bake for 30 mins. Remove foil and bake for another 5 minutes. Remove from the oven and let sit for 10 minutes before slicing.

Serve with remaining sauce and vegan parmesan on the side.

This fall favourite in our family has been veganized deliciously by Priya.

For my value pick I've chosen an Italian classic, Vernaccia di San Gimignano, from a hill town in Tuscany. It has been considered one of Italy's finest white wines since the Renaissance. This wine contrasts the richness of the lasagna as it's crisp and fresh with stone fruit and citrus notes while finishing with a mineral edge. It also has some texture and density, so it pairs well with the weight of the dish.

For my splurge pick I am recommending a Cabernet Franc from Canada in British Columbia's Okanagan Valley. The reds from the Southern Okanagan are rich and textured because of the climate, which is Canada's only desert. Cabernet Franc does particularly well here and develops rich, savoury notes without becoming too decadent, so it's able to keep its freshness. Here is an opportunity to enjoy that big red wine some of us love but are often hard to pair with plant-based food because of the tannins.

Pro Tip: *Add a bit of extra salt when finishing the lasagna if you're planning to enjoy it with a Cabernet Franc as it will help cut the tannins in the wine.*

LUCK 'O THE IRISH, BEEFLESS STEW

Serves 4 hearty portions

I felt like I had stumbled upon the luck 'o the Irish when I realized the jus from my Mushroom Wellington (see page 70) would make a dee-lish base for a beefless stew! I'd be willing to wager that you could serve this during any sports playoff game and none of your guests would guess that it's meatless. Serve with dinner rolls or homemade garlic bread. Mince fresh garlic into some plant-based butter and spread onto bread generously before toasting. Perfect and perfectly simple!

1 1/2 tbsp olive oil

3 medium shallots or 1 medium red onion, finely chopped

2-3 garlic cloves, minced

2 medium size potatoes, cut into bite sized cubes

2 medium carrots, cubed

1 cup dry Marsala or full-bodied red wine

2 cups vegan, beef-flavoured broth

1 1/2 tsp Herbes de Provence

1 bay leaf

1 cup faux beef strips, cut into bite-sized pieces

1 tbsp arrowroot flour or cornstarch, dissolved in 1/4 cup water

Salt and black pepper to taste

Sauté shallots in oil in a large pot over medium heat until translucent, 5-7 minutes. Add potatoes, carrots and garlic, cooking until veggies soften, about 3-5 minutes.

Add wine and let the veggies soak it up for another 3-5 minutes. Add the broth, Herbes de Provence and bay leaf and cook for 10-12 minutes. Stir in cornstarch/water mixture and beefless bits and cook for another 5 minutes.

Season to taste with salt (if needed, as the bouillon cubes may be salty enough) & pepper.

This hearty and warming stew will hit the spot on a wintry day.

For my value pick, look for a table wine from Spain based on the red Tempranillo grape, either on its own or blended with local varieties like Monastrell. You can usually find a decent one at a great price. These wines tend to be fruit forward yet slightly earthy with no oak treatment. They are a cheap and charming match to this stew.

For a splurge option try a Cabernet Sauvignon from Washington State, USA. These rich and bold wines can sometimes be a challenge to pair with vegan food, but it's a perfect match with this winter stew as all the robust flavours can stand up to the deep, cassis and dark berry notes of this elegant, yet bold red.

Pro Tip: *If the Cabernet is hard to find from Washington, a Western Australian Cabernet Sauvignon is equally as good.*

FARM TO TABLE POT PIE

Serves 6

The beauty of this dish is that it relies on pantry staples (onions, potatoes, carrots, and celery) but it can also be manipulated by using whatever veggies you have on hand, such as mushrooms, broccoli, beans, etc. As long as you keep some vegan pie crust in your freezer, you'll almost always be able to throw this together in a pinch. Be sure to chop all the veggies (and tofu or faux chicken, if using) into similar-sized pieces so they cook evenly.

2 vegan pie shells, thawed according to package instructions

2 tbsp olive oil

1 large onion, chopped

3-4 cloves garlic, minced

2 stalks celery

1 large carrot

2 cups cauliflower, small florets

2 medium potatoes, diced

1/2 cup white wine

1 cup sautéed faux chicken or firm tofu in bite-sized pieces (optional)

2 cups vegetable broth

1 tsp Herbes de Provence

1-2 tbsp flour or cornstarch

2 tbsp soy sauce or tamari sauce

Salt & pepper

Preheat the oven to 425 °F.

Bake the bottom pie crust in the preheated oven for 5-7 minutes so it doesn't get soggy during the main baking process.

Heat oil in a large frying pan over medium heat. Sauté onion and garlic for 2-3 minutes. Add vegetables and wine and cook for another 3-5 minutes. Add faux chicken, vegetable broth and Herbes de Provence.

Whisk cornstarch or flour with soy/tamari sauce and add to the pan. Bring to a boil then reduce to a simmer and cook until vegetables are just tender, about 5-7 minutes. You don't want the vegetables to overcook at this stage because they will continue to cook during baking and no one wants a mushy pie. Season with salt & pepper.

Pour the filling into the pie shell, placing the second shell on top and crimping the edges together. Cut a few slits in the top to let air escape during baking. Bake for 30 minutes.

For me, this is a perfect Sunday family dinner served with a side salad and something delicious to drink.

My value pick is a white wine from the Rioja region in Spain. These whites are based on the Garnacha Blanca grape and are very interesting and unique with round texture and contrasting bright acidity. White Riojas are reminiscent of Chardonnay when it comes to style. The fattiness and weight match the flaky crust beautifully and the broth Priya uses in this (the magic jus) works with the delicate nature of this wine.

My splurge wine is a white wine made from Chardonnay in Burgundy, France. While these white wines can be very expensive there is much value to be found in Mâconnais. Look for wines from the villages of St.Véran, Pouilly Fuissé and Pouilly-Vinzelles to explore slightly richer Chardonnays. Ideally these whites have some bottle age, roughly 5-6 years is perfect.

Pro Tip: *For either of these wines, don't serve ice cold as you will miss the nuances of what makes these wines so special. Serve in Burgundy glasses or any large wine glass you have on hand.*

BEYOND SHEPHERD'S PIE

Serves 6

Easily one of my ultimate comfort food meals, this pie is already full of veggies but adding a crisp salad or some sautéed greens is a nice way to round out the plate. It makes for a lovely, casual dinner party main course with a lot of satisfied smiles and 'mmm's'. For those who aren't fans of faux meat products I've given the option of substituting lentils or mushrooms.

FILLING

2 tbsp olive oil

1 large onion, diced

1 medium carrot, thickly sliced

2 stalks celery, thickly sliced

4-6 cloves garlic, roughly chopped

1/4 cup dry red wine (optional but recommended)

1 1/2 cups vegan ground round (you can replace this with more lentils and/or some sautéed mushrooms)

1 cup canned or cooked lentils

1/4 cup vegetable broth

1 tsp Herbes de Provence

2-3 tbsp low sugar ketchup blended with equal parts vegetable broth

1/2 cup steamed or canned corn kernels

1/2 tsp salt (only if your broth is salt-free)

1/4 tsp ground pepper

TOPPING

1 tsp salt

2 large potatoes, diced (peeled or not, your preference)

1/2 large cauliflower, roughly chopped

1 1/2-2 tbsp vegan margarine (add more for a creamier topping)

1/4 cup unsweetened non-dairy milk of choice

MAKE THE FILLING

Heat oil in a medium pot over medium heat. Add onions, carrots and celery and cook for 7-10 minutes until soft and translucent.

Add garlic and wine, cooking until veggies are soft and wine is absorbed, about 5 minutes. If using mushrooms, add at this point.

Add ground round and/or lentils, vegetable broth, Herbes de Provence and ketchup/broth blend, cooking for another 3-5 minutes. Taste and add more ketchup, or salt if needed to balance the flavours.

Add corn, stir until well-combined and pour mixture into an 8" square casserole.

MAKE THE TOPPING

Preheat the oven to 375 °F.

Add salt to about 1 inch of water in a medium pot and bring to a boil. Add potatoes and cauliflower, and steam for 8-10 minutes until vegetables are tender but not mushy. Drain. Add margarine and non-dairy milk and mash together. Season with more salt if needed. Spoon over the mixture in the casserole and run a fork along the top, simply for presentation's sake.

Bake for 25-30 minutes. Remove from the oven and let sit for 10 minutes before serving.

I grew up on my grandmas Shepherd's Pie, so successfully conquering this into a delicious vegan version makes me extremely happy. To me, this is a dish that you can serve to family and guests alike, come a Tuesday or Saturday night. And this dish calls for red wine, served in a large glass.

My value recommendation would be a lighter style Shiraz from Adelaide Hills in Southern Australia. These rich, heart-warming reds offer loads of red fruit flavours with distinct spicy notes that play off the warmth of this pie, leaving you wanting more of everything. The Adelaide Hills region is a cooler pocket in a warm area, so the wines keep their freshness and don't become too big to match with this dish.

My splurge wine would be a Southern Rhone blend, a Châteauneuf-du-Pape, which hails from a historic and very romantic place in Southern France. This riper style wine is based on the Grenache and Syrah grape but are ultimately blends of several grapes. They offer notes of fresh rosemary and lavender which grow wild in the region, along with some earthiness and red fruity tones. They are complex and will age well in your cellar. Note that different producers will use different amounts of the permissible grape varieties, creating many house styles. Find your favourite.

Pro Tip: *Don't be afraid to put a slight chill on these reds - bring them down to cellar temperature and serve them in large, generous glasses.*

MUSHROOM WELLINGTON WITH MADEIRA JUS

Serves 6

This is a showstopper main course. It's elegant, impressive and perfect for a holiday dinner party. I'm not gonna lie, it is time-consuming but on the flip side, it's not at all difficult. I like to use a blend of mushrooms, the more variety the better. You can omit the faux beef altogether but if you do, be sure to increase the amount of mushrooms and include portobello mushrooms in your mixture to add that 'meaty' texture.

MUSHROOM WELLINGTON

4-6 garlic cloves, minced

3 medium shallots, finely chopped

1 1/2 tbsp olive oil

1/4 cup dry Madeira, Marsala or full-bodied red wine

4 cups mixed mushrooms, not-too-thinly sliced

1 1/2 tsp Herbes de Provence

Salt & pepper

1 cup faux beef strips, cut into bite-sized pieces

1 package vegan puff pastry, thawed according to package directions

MADEIRA JUS

2 tbsp olive oil

1 large shallot, minced

1 cup dry Madeira, Marsala or full-bodied red wine

1/2 tsp Herbes de Provence

3 cups vegan 'beef' flavoured broth (available at health food stores)

1 bay leaf

1 tbsp arrowroot flour or cornstarch dissolved in 1/4 cup water

Black pepper to taste

MAKE THE WELLINGTON

Preheat the oven to 350 °F.

Sauté shallots in oil over medium heat until translucent, about 5-7 minutes. Add mushrooms and garlic, cooking until mushrooms soften, 3-5 minutes. Let the mushrooms sweat out and be sure to cook off all their liquid before adding the wine and 'beef' bits. Cook until wine is almost completely evaporated but don't let the mixture get dry. Add Herbes de Provence and cook until mushrooms start to brown. Season to taste with salt & pepper.

Roll out puff pastry dough into a large rectangle. Fill in the centre with the mushroom mixture. Fold long ends over first, followed by the short ends and seal with a crimp. Place with seam-side down on a baking sheet or dish and refrigerate for 15-20 minutes.

Bake the Wellington for 15-20 minutes or until it's a nice golden-brown. Remove from the oven and let rest for 10 minutes so it holds well together when cutting. Use a serrated knife as it will slice without squishing the pastry.

MAKE THE MADEIRA JUS

While the Wellington is in the oven, heat oil over medium heat in a medium pot. Add shallots and sauté until translucent. Add wine and cook for 5-7 minutes until the liquid reduces slightly. Add 'beef' broth, bay leaf, Herbes de Provence and black pepper. Cook for 15-20 minutes.

Add the cornstarch/water blend, bring to a boil and then reduce heat and simmer until sauce has thickened slightly, about 3-5 minutes. Sauce is not meant to be thick like a gravy so be careful not to overcook! Serve sauce in a gravy boat alongside the Wellington.

We have found this wonderful, wintry dish to work with both red and white wines.

My favourite value wine is a Beaujolais made from the red Gamay grape coming from France. These reds have little tannin (the mouth puckering feeling you get with astringency) and loads of red fruit flavours with fresh herb notes. What is wonderful about them is they pair so well with food; their acidity is fresh for a red wine and they are not heavy at all. You don't need to spend lots of money to get a Cru Beaujolais and it can be fun to check out the ten different villages and styles from them.

My splurge wine is a white from the Chardonnay grape in Sonoma County, California, USA. If you can find a Russian River Valley Chardonnay (the small area that helped put California on the map for this grape), even better. These whites are decadent, opulent and round with notes of toast and ripe apples. They work so well with Mushroom Wellington because Chardonnay loves to be paired with mushrooms and the creamy, even slightly buttery notes help echo the pastry while it all melts in your mouth.

Pro Tip: *You can serve Beaujolais chilled (great summer picnic wine) and it's a great segue red wine for those who normally prefer white wines. For both the Beaujolais and Chardonnay, I would recommend using a larger, rounder style of wine glass such as a Burgundy glass in order to experience the full flavor potential.*

SWEET TALK

Everyone is content, the big discussions are winding down but the party is not. Whether you stay around the dinner table or retire to more relaxed seating in the living room, the sweetness of good times is in the air and these desserts will put the perfect night cap on another evening well spent with friends and loved ones.

STICKY TOFFEE PUDDING

Serves 6

On an everyday basis I am more of a 'savoury over sweet' person but when the sweet tooth calls, it calls hard! Most sticky toffee pudding recipes use an overkill of sugar. Mine uses at least a cup less of sugar overall, but the depth of flavours in the cake, the toffee syrup and the candied pecans are so rich that you won't miss it. I know, I know, there are several steps to this dessert but it is not difficult, just a bit laborious and I guarantee that it will be worth the effort!

PUDDING

1 1/2 cups pitted dates (about 14-16 dates, I prefer Medjool because they're the softest and silkiest in texture)

1 cup canned coconut milk, well-stirred

2 cups unbleached all-purpose flour

1 tsp baking powder

1/2 tsp baking soda

1/2 tsp salt

1/2-3/4 tsp cinnamon

1/2 cup tightly packed brown sugar

1/2 cup canola or safflower oil (plus extra for greasing the pan)

2 tsp apple cider or white vinegar

1 tbsp vanilla extract

CANDIED PECANS

1/4 to 1/2 cup icing sugar

Pinch of sea salt

2 cups raw pecans, roughly chopped

2-4 tsp water

TOFFEE GLAZE

1 1/2 cups canned coconut milk, well stirred

3/4 cups brown sugar (preferably dark)

5 tbsp vegan margarine

1/4 tsp salt

MAKE THE PUDDING

Preheat the oven to 350 °F.

Place dates and coconut milk in a small pot. Bring to a gentle boil then reduce to a simmer and cook, covered, for 10 minutes. Remove from heat, mash dates and stir well, or blend in an upright blender until smooth, so that there are no clumpy bits of dates.

In a medium bowl whisk flour, baking powder, baking soda, salt and cinnamon. In a separate, larger bowl whisk the date mixture with brown sugar, oil, vinegar and vanilla. Add the flour mixture to the date mixture and blend slowly until just combined. Don't overmix, you know how finicky baking is!

Grease an 8-inch square baking pan lightly with oil. Fill the pan and bake for 18-20 minutes or until a toothpick inserted into the centre comes out relatively clean. It may still be moist but the toothpick should not be dripping in batter.

While the cake is baking, prepare the candied pecans.

MAKE THE PECANS

Toss the sugar and salt together. Add pecans and mix. Add water 1 teaspoon at a time, tossing until well coated, adding extra water if sugar isn't sticking to pecans. Spread onto a baking sheet and bake for 10-12 minutes Alternatively, you can put the pecans into the oven for the last 10-12 minutes of the pudding's bake time.

Remove pecans and pudding from the oven. Let cool while you prepare glaze.

MAKE THE GLAZE

In a medium pot combine all ingredients. Bring to a boil then reduce to medium-low heat and cook for 5-7 minutes, stirring occasionally until thickened.

Prick the pudding with a toothpick over the entire surface so the glaze can soak into it. Pour half of the glaze over the pudding top, letting it soak into the cake. Reserve the remainder to pour over individual servings, and top with candied pecans.

Serve and watch your guests swoon.

This is one of my all-time favourite desserts, reminding me of Christmas. This pudding is rich and flavourful so it can handle fuller, richer and sweeter styles of dessert wine.

The possibilities are endless, but I do love to play off the toffee notes in this dessert, so my value wine is a PX Sherry (Pedro Ximenez is the grape) from Spain. The wine itself has toffee, candied figs, dates and nut flavours along with a creamy texture. This is a match made in dessert heaven and can be found at a reasonable price.

An alternative wine is my splurge suggestion of a lovely German or Canadian Icewine. Icewine is costly to make as the grapes must stay on the vine until winter, and then whatever grapes are still there to pick after all the cute animals have been snacking on them, are pressed frozen creating liquid gold. Icewines age extremely well because they have a high amount of acidity and sugar. They can also develop candied fruit and honey notes with some bottle age.

Pro Tip: *I would serve the PX Sherry slightly chilled and the ice wine well chilled in a pretty little glass with about two fingers worth (or two ounces each).*

BASKET OF BERRIES SHORTCAKE

Serves 8

I grew up with strawberry shortcake. It was so popular that they even created an animated kids show based on the name! Whether you prefer strawberries, raspberries, blueberries or a mix of berries, this cake will be a showstopper. The coconut whipping cream is so light and fluffy, you may just choose to replace the real thing in all your cooking!

CAKE

1 1/2 cups all-purpose flour

2/3 cup sugar

1 tsp baking soda

1/8 tsp salt

1 cup almond milk

1/2 cup canola oil

1/8 cup apple cider vinegar

1 tbsp vanilla extract

1 1/2 cups berries of choice

COCONUT WHIPPING CREAM

1 can full fat coconut milk

1/4 cup icing sugar

Note: *Make sure your coconut milk is refrigerated overnight before using. I keep a couple of cans of coconut milk in my fridge at all times so I always have one when I need it.*

I also place my steel mixing bowl and the beater 'arms' in the freezer for 10 minutes just prior to using them as that helps the whipping cream to properly whip into the desired consistency.

MAKE THE COCONUT WHIPPING CREAM

Drain the can of coconut milk of any liquid. It is critical that you remove as MUCH liquid as possible or else your whipping cream won't actually whip. Believe me, it's happened to me and it can be very stressful!

Add coconut milk and icing sugar to a steel bowl. Whip using a hand beater at medium speed until all sugar is absorbed. Then increase speed to high and beat for 2-3 minutes until cream is slightly stiff so that peaks can be formed with a spoon. Refrigerate overnight.

MAKE THE CAKE

Preheat the oven to 350 °F.

Grease an 8 or 9-inch cake pan and line with parchment paper.

Whisk flour, sugar, baking soda and salt in a medium bowl. In a separate bowl whisk almond milk, oil, vinegar and vanilla. Pour the liquid mixture into the dry and whisk just until combined. Be careful not to overmix!

Pour batter into the pan and bake for 30-35 minutes, rotating halfway through baking time. Before you pull it out of the oven, be sure to do the tried and true toothpick test!

I like serving this cake 'deconstructed' and allowing guests to spoon the whipped cream and berries on themselves.

Hello summer berries! I love this dessert because it's so light, fluffy and fresh - it is summer in a dish! What I like about Priya's version is that it has all these qualities without lots of sugar.

Time to break out the Brachetto D'Acqui sparkling red wine from Northern Italy. These wines are very unique and pretty with a deep pink colour and fine bubbles. They have aromas of strawberry, cherry and raspberries and drink medium sweet, often with notes of honey and spice. Feel free to serve a few ounces in a snifter or a pretty cocktail glass to make this dessert into an event. I am only giving you one suggestion here because these are value driven wines and really are the best with this dessert!

Pro Tip: *If you can't find Brachetto, look for a local Pet-Nat wine (slightly sparkling and more natural style of wine). Any that are based off of a red grape will pair well with this!*

CHOCOLATE BOMB CAKES

Makes 12 cakes

These really are 'the bomb' in more ways than one. They create a chocolate explosion when you slice into them and the flavour is rich, deep and chocolatey. The recipe makes 12 which will come in handy for those guests who ask for a second serving!

Safflower, canola or coconut oil for greasing muffin tin

1 1/2 cups flour

2/3 cup sugar

1 tsp baking soda

1/2 tsp salt

1/3 cup unsweetened cocoa powder

1 cup unsweetened almond or rice milk

1/2 cup canola oil

2 tbsp apple cider vinegar

1 tbsp vanilla extract

1/2 cup dairy-free dark chocolate chips (or chocolate bar, chopped)

Garnish: Sliced strawberries, raspberries or bananas, and icing sugar

Preheat the oven to 350 °F. Lightly grease a 12-muffin pan.

In a large bowl, sift dry ingredients together. In a medium bowl, whisk wet ingredients.

Pour the wet mixture into the dry mixture and whisk until just combined.

Fill each muffin cup with 1 heaping tbsp of the batter. Drop 1 tsp of chocolate chips into each muffin and fill with remaining batter.

Bake for 12-15 minutes. Do not overcook or the chocolate will get absorbed into the cake.

Remove from the oven and let sit for a few minutes to firm up slightly. Run a knife around each cake and lift out gently. Serve with fresh fruit of choice and a dusting of icing sugar.

This dessert, while rich, is not overly sweet, giving us a few more options when it comes to pairing it with wine.

Be bold and try it with a California, USA red Zinfandel (table wine not dessert wine) for a value pick. Fruit forward and not tannic, these wines helped to put California on the wine map. They naturally have a bit of spice and wild red fruit which melds beautifully with the chocolate cake.

If you want to splurge, try an Italian Amarone della Valpolicella. These wines are made from dried grapes which concentrate the intensity of the wine flavours, showcasing dried red fruits or stewed red fruit notes. They're rich and bold but finish with a hint of bitterness playing off the dark chocolate for a truly special, and decadent end to a special meal.

Pro Tip: *While these are both not traditionally regarded as dessert wines, you can treat them as such and pour a few ounces only for this match. They can both range higher in alcohol as well so a few ounces goes a long way.*

SPICED APPLE BUNDT

Serves 8-10

It's New Year's Day and you're looking for a warm cake to serve at brunch. The spiced apple cake is a traditional favourite and the best part of this one is that it's not overly sweet. The combination of spices gives it such a 'wrapped in a blanket' feel. You can elevate this dessert by using the caramel sauce and spiced pecans from the Sticky Toffee Pudding recipe (see page 74).

2 1/4 cups unbleached all-purpose flour
2 tsp baking soda
1 1/2 tsp ground cinnamon
1 tsp salt
1/2 tsp each ground nutmeg, allspice, ginger
2 cups unsweetened applesauce
3/4 cup brown sugar
1/2 cup canola or safflower oil
1/4 cup white or apple-cider vinegar
1 tbsp pure vanilla extract
Icing sugar for dusting (optional)

Preheat the oven to 350 °F.

Lightly grease a bundt pan.

In a large bowl, whisk together flour, baking soda, salt, cinnamon, nutmeg, allspice and ginger.

In a smaller bowl, whisk together applesauce, brown sugar, oil, vinegar, and vanilla.

Pour the wet mixture into the dry mixture and whisk until just combined. Be careful not to overmix or the cake will turn out a bit gummy.

Pour batter evenly into a bundt pan, smoothing the top. Bake for 40 to 45 minutes, turning the pan at the halfway point for even cooking. Let the cake cool completely then slide a knife gently around the cake before unmolding.

Lightly dust with icing sugar.

This delicious and fragrant cake is not sweet, so we want to avoid traditional dessert style wines. Instead, for a value option, try an off-dry Riesling from Germany, Canada or New Zealand to play off that appley goodness.

For a splurge, I would invest in a lovely Gewurztraminer from Alsace. Look for Grand Crus which are still a relative bargain for what you get. These whites carry ginger and honeyed notes that work so well with the spices in this cake and really are a special match.

Pro Tip: *If you want to try something totally different, I suggest a high-quality cider with this for a cheeky match.*

PIÑA COLADA CAKE

Serves 6-8

There are a lot of 'pineapple upside-down cake' recipes out there so I decided to elevate this cake and turn it into an edible version of a favorite vacation drink, the piña colada. Why? Because pineapple and coconut are already a perfect pairing while the rum adds a lovely, deep and rich note to the final product. And also, why not?

TOPPING

1/4 cup vegan butter/margarine, melted

3/4 cup, packed brown sugar

1 can pineapple slices, reserving liquid for the Rum Syrup below

Maraschino cherries, if desired

CAKE

2 1/2 cups flour

1 cup sugar

1 1/2 tsp baking soda

3/4 tsp salt

1 cup shredded, unsweetened coconut

1 cup full-fat, canned coconut milk

Juice from the canned pineapple

1/2 cup melted coconut oil

1 tbsp apple cider vinegar

1 tsp vanilla

RUM SYRUP

3 tbsps vegan margarine or butter

1/4 tsp salt

1/2 cup dark rum

1 tbsp real maple syrup

1/2 tsp vanilla extract (add at end)

Shredded Coconut for garnish (optional)

MAKE THE TOPPING

Spread melted butter/margarine evenly across a 13x9-inch baking pan. Sprinkle brown sugar evenly over butter. Arrange pineapple slices on brown sugar, pressing down slightly. If using maraschino cherries, place them in the centre of each pineapple slice.

MAKE THE CAKE

Heat the oven to 350°F.

Sift the flour into a mixing bowl. Add the sugar, baking soda, salt and shredded coconut and whisk together well.

In a separate bowl whisk together the coconut milk, pineapple juice, melted coconut oil, vinegar, and vanilla.

Add wet ingredients to the dry ones and fold together with a wooden spoon. Be careful not to overmix.

Pour the batter into the pan and spread it out to the edges with the back of a spoon.

Bake for 30 minutes or until a toothpick inserted into the center of the cake comes out clean.

MAKE THE RUM SYRUP

While the cake is baking, combine the syrup ingredients, except vanilla in a medium-sized pot. Bring to a rapid boil then reduce to low and simmer for 8 to 10 minutes until the syrup reduces by a third. Remove from heat and stir in the vanilla.

Remove cake from the oven and run a knife around the edges and place a serving dish or cutting board on top. Invert the cake onto the serving dish but leave the pan on top of the cake so the brown sugar can soak into the cake.

Use a long toothpick to poke holes all over the cake, carefully avoiding the pineapple slices. Pour about 1/4 cup of the syrup evenly over the cake and allow it to soak in. Pour remaining syrup over the slices just before serving and top with a light sprinkle of shredded coconut, if desired.

My favourite drink as a cake?! What!! There's loads of coconut and a beautiful sweetness from the caramelized pineapple in this dessert.

This delightful cake is amazing with a luscious Sautérnes dessert wine from Bordeaux, France. Sautérnes is one of the original dessert wines of the world with its notes of dried apricots and honey. And while it's sweet, it has the perfect level of ripeness to work with this [one day] award winning dessert! You can find examples in the value category, but you're welcome to splurge here and spend more (the sky's the limit).

Pro Tip: *Great examples can be found that are cellar worthy and will improve and age for 20 plus years. This wine is a great investment!*

COCONUT CREAM PIE

Serves 6-8

When I was a kid, my mom and I would walk to the mall and go to the Kmart cafeteria for lunch and I would always have a slice of coconut cream pie. When I used to think back to those days it made me sad that I'd never enjoy a cool slice of creamy pie with my mom again. Well I'm happy to say that there is no more wistful thinking because here is a veganized version that will make everyone at your table wonder if you cheated and picked up a boxed pie from the freezer aisle!

CRUST

1 cup vegan graham cracker crumbs (e.g. Kinnikinnick brand)

3 tbsp vegan butter or margarine melted

FILLING

1 cup canned coconut milk

1/3 cup sugar

1/8 tsp salt

1 tbsp vanilla extract

1/2 cup shredded, unsweetened coconut

TOPPING

1 batch of Coconut Whipping Cream (see instructions in Basket Of Berries Shortcake recipe on page 76)

1/2 cup shredded, unsweetened coconut, toasted in the oven until lightly browned

MAKE THE CRUST

Combine crumbs and butter or margarine and press onto the bottom of a 9-inch round baking pan. Bake at 350 °F for 10 mins or until golden but not burnt!

MAKE THE FILLING

In a medium pot, add coconut milk, sugar and salt over medium-high heat. Whisk until the mixture starts to boil. Then reduce heat to medium and drizzle the cornstarch/almond milk slowly into the pot, whisking continuously. Cook for 5 minutes or so, whisking often and scraping down the sides, until it reaches a pudding-like consistency. Remove from heat before adding vanilla extract and shredded coconut. Let cool for a few minutes.

ASSEMBLE

Pour the filling mixture into the prepared crust. Let it cool at room temperature completely, then cover with plastic wrap and chill in the refrigerator for at least 6 hours or overnight.

When ready to assemble,, top the chilled pie with the coconut whipping cream and use a narrow spatula or butter knife to create peaks. Sprinkle with the toasted, shredded coconut and chill for 10-15 minutes before serving.

We love a well-made Riesling and it seems like anything with coconut does too! While you can certainly enjoy this dessert sans vino, I like to use a bit of left-over Riesling from dinner and enjoy the last sips of it with this pie. My value wine would be an off-dry Riesling from Niagara, Ontario, Canada. These whites are zippy and fresh with lots of stone fruit flavors and even a bit of honey. They have enough sweetness to balance the pie but won't overwhelm it. Ontario's cool climate has become known for the excellent Rieslings it can produce.

My splurge wine would be a 'single vineyard' German off-dry Riesling from the Mosel growing area which offers low alcohol partnered with mouth quenching acidity and some sweetness. These top German whites are known for offering up serious complexity and are incredibly age worthy (think up to 80 years old), ..but who can wait?!

Pro Tip: *These Rieslings can literally work through an entire meal. They make a great aperitif wine, are very versatile with food (great with spicy food, an nt alternative to beer with Indian food) and, because of the lower alcohol level, you can enjoy even more.*

"THE PERFECT TART" LEMON CAKE

Serves 8

Many lemon cakes are too tart for me. My version strikes a balance between sweet and sour. This cake is perfect for a summer dinner on the back deck and you might be surprised by Jen's pairing suggestion! I find that using maple syrup or agave instead of sugar in the curd makes for a nicer texture and flavour. Try not to eat all the curd before you get around to assembling the cake as it's quite delicious on its own!

LEMON CURD

1/4 cup unsweetened almond milk

3 tbsp arrowroot powder or cornstarch

1/4 cup maple syrup or agave

Zest and juice of 1 large lemon

1/2 tsp turmeric (optional to add more of a yellow colour)

CAKE

2 and 2/3 cups all purpose flour

1 cup sugar

1 1/2 tsp baking soda

3/4 tsp Salt

1 1/2 cups unsweetened soy or almond milk

1/2 cup canola or safflower oil

1 tbsp apple cider vinegar

1 tsp vanilla extract

2 tsp lemon extract

2 tbsp Lemon Zest

1/4 tsp turmeric for color (optional)

MAKE THE LEMON CURD

Over medium high heat, whisk water and arrowroot or cornstarch in a small pot until fully dissolved.

Bring to a boil, stirring constantly as the mixture begins to thicken, about 3 minutes. Slowly drizzle in the maple syrup/agave and continue stirring. Cook on low heat for another minute until well combined. Curd should be thick and spreadable.

Remove from heat. Add lemon juice & zest and mix well. Whisk in the turmeric if using and then refrigerate to cool until ready to use. The curd can be made in advance and kept in the fridge for up to 3 days.

MAKE THE CAKE

Preheat the oven to 350 °F.

Lightly grease two 8-inch round cake pans or line the bottoms with parchment paper.

Sift the flour into a mixing bowl and add sugar, baking soda and salt. Then add the non-dairy milk, oil, vinegar, vanilla and lemon extracts and lemon zest. Whisk until combined.

Divide the batter between the two cake pans and bake for 25-30 minutes. Test with a toothpick after 25 minutes to see if it's done, you don't want the edges to burn.

Remove the cakes from the pans and cool completely before layering with the lemon curd.

Spread half the curd on the bottom layer of cake, add the second cake layer and top with remaining curd. Decorate with thin slices of lemon, fresh blueberries, or flowers.

Oh yum, a moist cake with custard and lemon, bring it on! This screams spring to me, so I want to pair it with fresh and floral wines.

For my value pick, I'm recommending a Moscato d'Asti from Northern Italy. This is a light, slightly sparkling sweet wine with low alcohol and delicate floral notes. While Priya and I often refer to this wine as 'breakfast wine', it works amazingly with the lemony sweet and tart notes of this cake, keeping everything fresh and springlike.

For my splurge wine I am staying in Italy but moving further South to the Soave region and pairing this dessert with a Recioto di Soave DOCG. This dessert wine is created by leaving the grapes on the vine to dry out and concentrate by way of water evaporation. This process creates lush and sweet wines that are flavour packed and delicately floral. If you are going for this option, add a teaspoon of it into the custard when making it.

Pro Tip: *Serve these Italian wonders in very pretty glasses, think flutes or dainty antique glasses.*

OH-SO-GOOEY PECAN SQUARES

Makes 9-12 squares, depending on how large you cut them

Nothing says 'holidays' like gooey pecans resting atop a shortbread crust! They feel like a distant cousin to my sticky toffee pudding recipe but these squares have the lovely, salty crispiness of shortbread in place of the soft, dense cake. It's a dessert you'll always find at my holiday cocktail party.

CRUST

1 1/2 cups all-purpose flour

1/4 cup sugar

1/4 tsp salt

1/2 cup vegan margarine

TOPPING

1/2 cup brown sugar (not packed)

4 tbsp vegan margarine

1/4 cup plus 2 tbsp agave or maple syrup

1/2 cup canned, full fat coconut milk

2 tbsp cornstarch

2 cups pecans, lightly toasted and roughly chopped

1 tsp vanilla extract

MAKE THE CRUST

Preheat the oven to 350 °F.

Line the bottom of an 8-inch square baking dish with parchment paper.

In a bowl, sift together dry ingredients. Add the margarine in with a fork or whisk. Mixture should be crumbly but hold together when you squeeze it with your fingers. Press into a baking dish and bake for 20-25 minutes.

Remove and let cool while preparing the topping.

MAKE THE TOPPING

Whisk together coconut milk and cornstarch. Set aside.

Combine the sugar, margarine and agave or maple syrup in a small pot over medium heat. Stir until margarine has completely dissolved. Add coconut milk/cornstarch mixture and bring to a boil, then reduce heat and simmer for 5 minutes or until it's thickened and is no longer runny.

Remove from heat and stir in vanilla and pecans. Spread evenly over the shortbread and bake for 12-15 minutes until the topping has firmed up. Let cool completely then chill in the fridge for 3 hours or overnight to let the filling set.

Run a sharp knife around the edges of the baking dish and cut into squares of desired size before carefully lifting the pieces out.

This dessert is such a delicious indulgence that only gets better with a delectable dessert wine.

My value pick is the interesting Palo Cortado Sherry from Spain. This is a historic and legendary wine that starts its life as a Fino sherry but with a twist of fate evolves into this special, nutty and rich wine. It's a pick that punches way above its weight based on its affordable price.

My splurge choice may be a bit surprising to you, a Bourbon whiskey. Bourbon is barrel-aged and made mostly of corn hailing from Kentucky, USA. The nutty pecans and sweet shortbread crust compliment the caramel notes in the whiskey and are a perfect match.

Pro Tip: *Both recommendations are higher in alcohol, so serve only about an ounce.*

TIRAMISU

Serves 6-8

Here's a decadent dessert that I've always loved, but that somehow seemed too complicated to make at home. Not so! It's surprisingly easy. The only trick, really, is in the vegan mascarpone, which takes a bit of patience. You can choose to make individual servings in pretty parfait bowls or make a full tiramisu in a trifle dish. It's best served after sitting in the fridge for a few hours so keep that in mind!

Note: *It helps to chill your mixing bowl and beaters for about 10 minutes in the freezer right before using.*

CAKE

1 1/2 cups all purpose flour

3/4 cup sugar

1 tsp baking powder

1/2 tsp salt

3/4 cup non-dairy milk of choice

1/2 cup canola oil

2 tbsp apple cider vinegar

1 tbsp almond extract

MASCARPONE

1 cup raw cashews, soaked in water for 30 mins

3/4 cup powdered sugar

1/2 cup non-dairy milk of choice

1 tsp vanilla extract

1 x 14 oz can full-fat coconut milk, chilled overnight in the fridge

COFFEE SOAK

1 cup very strong coffee or espresso, at room temperature (use decaf if you prefer)

2 tbsp dark rum, coffee liqueur or almond liqueur (depending on what flavour you'd like to enhance)

GARNISH

1/4 cup dark cocoa powder

Shaved, dark chocolate

MAKE THE CAKE

Preheat the oven to 350 °F.

Whisk together all the dry ingredients in a large bowl.

Whisk liquid ingredients in a small bowl. Pour wet mixture into the dry mixture and blend together until combined, without overmixing.

Pour into a lightly greased, 9-inch square baking pan. Bake for 25-30 minutes, being careful not to let the edges brown too much—you don't want crispy edges.

Remove from the oven and let the cake cool completely.

MAKE THE MASCARPONE

Add the cashews, sugar, non-dairy milk and vanilla extract to a blender and blend until completely smooth, scraping down the sides often.

Drain all liquid from the can of coconut milk , leaving only the hardened cream. Add the cream to a mixing bowl and mix with a hand beater until it softens and becomes fluffy. Gently fold in the cashew mixture with a spatula. Chill in the fridge for at least an hour until ready to use.

MAKE THE COFFEE SOAK

Mix the coffee and rum or liqueur together.

ASSEMBLY

Cut the cake into 1 inch cubes, slightly smaller if making individual portions. Use half the cubes as the first layer.

Drench with half of the coffee soak. I use a brush to do this so I can get an even soak. Layer half of the coconut mascarpone next and dust with half the cocoa powder. Add remaining cake cubes, top with remaining mascarpone and finish with an even dusting of cocoa powder and the chocolate shavings.

Chill cake in the fridge for at least a few hours, if not overnight, to let the coffee soak through and all the flavours to combine.

I love this dessert and its creaminess coupled with those mascarpone notes.

My favourite match to this is an Oloroso Sherry from Spain. These nutty and creamy wines are classic fortified wines made in Jerez and produced by oxidative aging techniques. They are exceptional and often overlooked in the world of wine matching. Serve with a slight chill.

EASY SWAPS AND ADDITIONS TO YOUR PANTRY

I went vegan for a myriad of reasons but the main one was that I could no longer rationalize my love for animals with the fact that I was contributing to their suffering and ultimately, their death. The decision, once made, was easy to stick to in my personal life but since I've always been a hostess at heart, I had to learn to adapt so that I could still host fabulous dinners and cocktail parties.

My approach to cooking is to do the best you can and buy the best quality products your lifestyle permits. If you want and are able to buy organic produce and the best, artisanal vanilla extract, spices and cooking oils and that's within your means, fabulous! But just as we don't open a $100 bottle of wine for dinner every night, we don't need to pull out the top-level ingredients for dinner every night either. There's nothing wrong in saving that artisanal vanilla and top-shelf olive oil for a special occasion and sticking with the regular products in your pantry for everyday use.

For me and for many of you who will try these recipes, time is often a major factor. We work, we have a home to clean, we have babies and/or fur babies to take care of and our time is precious. My goal with these recipes is to make them accessible so you don't have to soak dried beans overnight for a recipe or make your own mayonnaise from scratch.

All that to say that with the exception of a few elaborate recipes, most of the dishes in this book are fairly simple even when they have many steps.

What I discovered is that there are several spices and ingredients that have flavours mimicking some animal-based foods such as cheese, eggs and fish.

In addition to a well-stocked pantry in terms of spices and canned goods, here is a list of my vegan essentials in various categories.

Canned Goods

COCONUT CREAM
Full-fat cans are used to make coconut whipping cream while lighter versions can be used in Thai curries and in baking.

Tip: *keep a few cans of full fat cans in the fridge so they're always ready when you want to make some coconut whipped cream!*

CANNED LENTILS
Small, brown lentils can be used as a substitute for ground beef in recipes such as Shepherd's Pie.

CANNED JACKFRUIT IN BRINE
This is an amazing replication of pulled pork. Just make sure you don't accidentally pick up the type that is preserved in syrup.

Spices

BLACK SALT
Strangely-named since the salt is actually pink, but it provides an egg-like flavour to dishes such as scrambled tofu.

HERBES DE PROVENCE
A blend of spices that does heavenly things for mushrooms and savoury meals like Shepherd's Pie.

OLD BAY SEASONING
Provides a seafood flavour to dishes such as chickpea tuna pockets and Vegan Crab Cakes.

SAFFRON
The world's most expensive spice has delicate, floral notes and surprisingly, is a libido enhancer. So double your pleasure!

CAJUN SPICE BLEND
Gives that Tex-Mex flavour to chili and other Southern or Latin-inspired dishes.

Other flavour enhancers

NUTRITIONAL YEAST
One of the unappetizing-sounding ingredients that imparts a 'cheesy' taste to recipes like macaroni and cheese.

NORI OR OTHER SEAWEED
Provide 'sea' or 'fishy' notes to dishes and is a great source of iodine and Vitamin K which many vegans lack.

CANNED CHILIS IN ADOBO SAUCE
Adds a blend of heat, sweetness and smoky depth to Latin dishes.

TAMARI SAUCE
A good soy sauce substitute for those with gluten issues.

SESAME OIL
Used often in Asian dressings and sauces.

COCONUT OIL
I primarily use it for baking however many people like to use this as their main cooking oil as it has a high smoke point which makes it a good oil for frying. However, it is almost 6 times higher in saturated fat than olive oil.

CANOLA OIL FOR BAKING

LIQUID SMOKE
Just a few drops can add wonderful smoky flavours to dishes.

WHITE MISO PASTE
Adds depth and 'umami' to Asian dishes and dressings. Less salty and more pungent than it's red cousin.

BALSAMIC VINEGAR
My go-to for salad dressing aside from fresh lemon juice. Did you know that balsamic vinegar is made from grapes? Traditional balsamic vinegar is still only made in Reggio Emilia and Modena, Italy and is quite expensive. The bottles you see on most grocery store shelves are either blended with wine vinegar or are purely wine vinegar with colouring and other flavouring agents to mimic traditional balsamic vinegar.

COCOA POWDER

PURE VANILLA EXTRACT
As opposed to artificial or imitation vanilla flavouring.

Other items

RAW CASHEWS AND ALMONDS
Great to create plant-based 'cream' sauces and 'cheesy' fillings (such as the filling used in the jalapeno poppers recipe).

RAW (UNSALTED) PEANUTS, WALNUTS AND PECANS
If you need toasted nuts for a recipe it's best to do it yourself. Raw nuts are usually called for in baking.

ROASTED PUMPKIN SEEDS, SUNFLOWER SEEDS AND HEMP SEEDS
Can be used separately or together as a protein-packed topping for salads, rice and soups.

Faux Meats & Soy Products

ITALIAN-STYLE AND SPICY SAUSAGES

GROUND 'BEEF'

'BEEF' CHUNKS / 'CHICKEN' CHUNKS

TOFU IN A VARIETY OF TEXTURES
Soft tofu is great as a ricotta substitute or to blend into cream sauces and dressings. Medium and firm options are good for scrambles or for recipes like the Spinach Artichoke Dip. Extra firm is best for stir fry dishes or to bake for a more dense, 'meaty' texture.

FOR THE SUSTAINABLY-MINDED HOST

Natural Place Settings

As the saying goes, 'bring the outdoors, in' by using produce to set the table. Have you ever seen a brussel sprout stalk? It's gorgeous and would make for a unique centrepiece. Or try those mini pumpkins as candle holders and then 'recycle' them as treats for squirrels and birds.

Ahh the table centrepiece. I love to bring the outside in with flowers or bunches of fresh herbs from the garden in the summer, to sprigs of evergreen boughs and pinecones in the winter. When we were kids we'd collect seashells and rocks and somewhere along the way we decided that was childish. Why? They can add such lovely accents to your home and table decor.

There are so many creative ways to reuse corks from wine bottles. My favourites are to collect all the corks from special bottles you've enjoyed and turn them into a wreath, or use them for your dining or buffet table as place card holders.

Sure recycling is great but why throw away all those lovely glass jars when you can reuse them in a myriad of ways? From storing dried goods in your pantry to using as candleholders and vases, there are so many creative things you can do, all while saving the planet by keeping those jars from being washed and recycled.

Chilling Wine in a Jiffy

We've all been there, an impromptu dinner with a friend and no chilled wine (note to self: ALWAYS have a bottle of white and rosé in the fridge)! I always keep frozen grapes on hand because they'll cool your beverage quickly and without imparting any flavour.

Plus, grapes in grapes? There's something fun and trippy about that!

Scrap That

Food waste is a huge problem in the world. Composting is obviously the go-to option and we've become so used to it that we toss our scraps into the compost without thinking. Sometimes, however, we throw away a bit too much. Here is a list of veggies and herbs that will make a nice stock. Keep the peels and ends and store in a ziploc until you have a bag full enough to brew a pot of stock:

Potatoes, carrots, onions, garlic, mushrooms, celery, herbs in small quantities (cilantro, basil, parsley, thyme, rosemary).

Careful to avoid bitter items such as cruciferous veggies, and items like beets which will result in purple broth. Not so great in your risotto!

COOKING WITH WINE

I love that fridge magnet that shows a 1950's housewife holding a glass of wine beside a stove with a caption that reads, 'I like cooking with wine, sometimes I even put some in the food!'. I actually do put wine in my food, quite often in fact, and I don't always want to open a bottle just for the 1/2 cup I may need for a recipe. That's why I freeze leftover wine (haha, 'leftover wine'!) in an ice cube tray so I always have some on hand.

When cooking with wine, here are some basic rules:

Be conscious of colour--red wine is great for adding deep, rich notes but it will also change the colour of your dish so you may not want to use it in cream sauces for example. Generally speaking, white wines are great for lighter colour dishes while red are great for tomato-based sauces, gravies and hearty stews or chili.

Be aware of sugar levels. You don't want to use a sweet wine in a savoury dish. I've specified in some recipes to use a dry Marsala wine for this reason, because Marsala wines can be super sweet and that would obviously affect the final dish. I tend to use whatever is open but if there isn't a bottle on the counter, then I'll choose an inexpensive bottle, no need to feel you must spend a lot for a wine you're cooking with.

At the same time, if the recipe only calls for 1/2 a cup or so, you want to be able to enjoy drinking the rest of the bottle! I like dry, crisp, fairly acidic whites such as Pinot Grigio or Sauvignon Blanc. Avoid big, oaky Chardonnay, or sweeter Rieslings and Gewürztraminers.

For reds, I prefer rich, full-bodied wines such as Merlot or Malbec. These wines aren't super tannic either which is important in vegan cooking because tannins interact with fats and protein and those are very different in plant-based dishes from their animal-based counterparts. Avoid big, tannic bombs like certain Cabernet Sauvignons, Syrahs and Barolos.

Another option is to look at the wine pairing and if the recipe calls for wine, see if you can use some from the bottle you'll be serving with the dish as it will meld the flavours for an even more perfect pairing. It's always a good idea to keep a few inexpensive bottles on hand for when you may need a wee bit to dress up a meal!

A big rule of thumb--if you wouldn't drink the wine because it's gone 'off' or has been open for a long time, don't cook with it. A tainted or past-its-date wine will be noticeable in the dish.

In terms of when to add the wine, I generally add it early on, when the onions and garlic are softening. This allows the wine to soak in the for the most flavour impact. Adding wine towards the end of the cooking time will result in a more wine-forward taste, with the wine overpowering the other elements in the dish.

Adding the wine early also gives time for much of the alcohol to burn off. Keep in mind that the idea of all the alcohol evaporating is a bit of a myth unless you're slow-cooking or simmering your dish for hours!

FOOD & WINE MATCHING PRINCIPLES

I am suspecting you have experienced at least a few wine and food pairings that were perfectly matched, as well as a few that were, let's say, not so great.

The idea, of course, is to wind up with a match that elevates both the food and wine, as well as the entire experience. With a little knowledge, you can help take the guesswork out of what pairs best together.

Now remember, we all have our own personal likes, dislikes and sensitivities to different spices, textures and flavours so bear that in mind - that preference is queen and as always, this is a judgement free zone.

Here are a few general concepts to consider when it comes to pairing wine with your meals.

'What grows together goes together'

This saying comes from Europe where the cultivation of grapes for wine flourished. The idea here is that people would eat very locally and then drink the wines that were locally produced. Now, of course, we have a much wider choice of foods and global cuisines, and we also have wines being grown all over the world. With that said, I still like this concept as it goes back to the idea of the '100-mile diet' and supporting local farmers.

Matching through the weight of the wine

This concept is based on matching either the textures or weight of the dish to that of the wine. For example, think of a light, fresh spring salad working well with a light, fresh and delicate white wine. If you're curious about opposing weights, think of a heavy, rich bean stew with a light and low tannin red wine. You can also work this in reverse by using a light crisp wine with a heavy dish.

Sweet and Salty

For people who enjoy this combination (think Chicago Mix popcorn), it's fun to play around with the idea when it comes to food and wine matching. For example, try an off-dry wine with salted popcorn or chips.

Acid and Fat

Foods heavy in oils such as avocado, nuts or coconut can partner very well with wines that are higher in acidity such as an Alsatian Riesling or a Chablis, both from France. The crisp acid in the wine cuts through the natural fat and cleanses your palate. Another example I love is hummus with excellent olive oil, crisp crackers and Grüner Veltliner from Austria.

Matching or contrasting flavours

This idea revolves around the flavours in the food that can be copied by or contrasted by the flavours in the wine. Consider a smoky, spicy Mediterranean dish being matched by a smoky, spicy wine such as a Syrah from Northern Rhône, France. Or you may use a contrasting wine that has some sweetness and more focused fruit flavors such as a soft and juicy Merlot from California paired with the smoky, spicy Mediterranean dish.

Classic Matches

Most of our classic references for matching food and wine are with animal fats and proteins. For example, chèvre goat cheese from the Loire Valley matched with a Sancerre wine from the Loire. I have generally found that when you swap out the meat-based dish for a vegan substitute, the classic pairings for the dish tend to work (you can always adjust salt/acid in the dish to work around).

With that said, there are a few classic pairings that are plant-based, and I am having fun creating my own new classics. Try Spanish olives and nuts with Manzanilla Sherry, or white asparagus with a German Riesling. Fungi-based dishes pair well with earthy Pinot Noir and bean-based dishes have an affinity with dry Rosé. Try quinoa-based salads with earthy Alsatian Pinot Gris and cashew cream sauces with a buttery Chardonnay.

The idea is to have fun, experiment and find those perfect pairings. What follows are things to take into consideration when matching plant-based foods with wine. These tips can help make the most of both, your meal and your wine.

MATCHING PRINCIPLES: THINGS TO CONSIDER IN FOOD

Sweetness

Sweetness can increase the perception of bitterness, astringency, acidity and alcohol in the wine. The general rule of thumb is to choose a wine that has a higher level of sweetness than the food does.

Umami

Umami can be difficult to isolate as it's usually intertwined with other flavours in the food. Umami tends to increase the flavour in the food even more (for example, it makes salty food taste even more salty). This can increase the perception of bitterness, astringency, acidity and the warming effect of alcohol in a wine, so avoid high acid and youthful tannic wines (like young Barolo or California Cabernet).

You can find high levels of umami in lots of plant-based foods such as cooked and dried mushrooms, tofu, tomatoes and miso paste. The addition of salt can help these foods pair better with wines, especially those wines that have higher levels of tannins and therefore bitterness. A great solution is to partner an aged version of the wine (for example an older Barolo) and ensure that there is enough salt in the dish.

Acidity

Acidity increases the perception of body, sweetness and fruitiness in a wine. High acid foods pair well with high acid wines and tend to enhance the fruitiness of the wine. Likewise, wines that have lower acidity make poor partners to high acid foods because they can taste flat or flabby.

Chili Heat

Spice increases the perception of bitterness, astringency, acidity, and the burning effect of alcohol. In other words, low alcohol wines or even beers with some sweetness can really offset the effects of heat in food. Using wines with both sweetness and low alcohol can help neutralize the chili heat.

Salt

Salt can decrease the perception of astringency, bitterness and acid in a wine, and increase the perception of body. Salt is our friend, especially with the tannic red wines as it reduces the perception of tannins in the wine, allowing you to enjoy the wine without any animal proteins. Remember it's always easier to adjust up on the salt, so don't go overboard and check the pairing closer to serving it.

Bitterness

Quite simply, bitterness in the food can increase bitterness in the wine. The next time you make an arugula and radicchio salad, think of a wine that does not exhibit bitterness as these flavours will only compound. For example, you wouldn't pair a California Cabernet Sauvignon with an arugula and radicchio salad, instead you might opt for a Grüner Veltliner.

Cooking Method

The way food is prepared can go a long way in how it will work with wine. Consider this, is your dish mostly raw/fresh and crunchy? If so, grab a wine that naturally echoes this such as an Albariño from Spain. Are you adding smoke/barbeque grilled notes? If so, try a Northern Rhône Syrah or Southern Rhône's Châteauneuf-du-Pape. Does the dish include a sauce with a dominate flavour? If so, look for a wine that can compliment or contrast it. The idea here is the end flavour of the dish can be influenced greatly by cooking method and is worth consideration.

DOES THE GLASS MATTER?

This is a question I get all the time: do I need to spend the money on good crystal wine glasses, and do I need to have several different types? Since there is no easy answer, it's ultimately up to you what you like and want to spend, however, I wanted to give you a bit of insight that I have gained over the years.

Let's begin with how you would taste a wine, which starts with smell. Did you know your nose has about 40 million olfactory receptors? You have the ability to distinguish over 10,000 scents, especially with training, and wine can have hundreds and hundreds of different aromas. Since we know tasting wine starts with smelling the wine, the logic of having a particular glass that allows you to narrow in on the specific wine's aromas would make sense.

I recognize not everyone may agree with this, but for me, how you experience a wine can be elevated by the right glass. Putting a great wine in a poorly made glass will reduce the appreciation of it. With that said, putting a poorly made wine in a great glass will not make the wine taste better, sadly.

Let's examine the architecture of a wine glass.

You have the base, the stem, the bowl and the lip. The format of the bowl will showcase the aromas by intensifying them as it will allow you to swirl the wine and volatize the aromas within it.

White wines with delicate floral aromas like Riesling will be best showcased in a smaller glass that allows the aromas to improve and helps to maintain a cooler temperature. White wines that benefit from larger bowls are oak-aged Chardonnays, Viogniers, aged White Riojas, and orange wines.

For red wines, a larger and more square shaped or oval bowl tends to work, especially for Bordeaux varietals such as Cabernet Sauvignon and Merlot. Medium to full-bodied reds such as Syrah, Malbec and Zinfandel do well in these glasses too. For grapes such as Pinot Noir, Gamay, Nebbiolo or Valpolicella, the go-to would be a wide round bowl to best display the aromatics.

I personally prefer stemmed glasses, because by holding the base or stem of the glass, there are no fingerprints nor am I heating up the wine with my hand.

The best crystal glasses can be expensive because they are made of hand-blown lead crystal. So, if you do splurge, treat them with care. I recommend hand washing and polishing yourself. Consider where you store them because they can pick up aromas (so avoid the spice cupboard or cardboard boxes)

Ultimately my recommendation is to pick a few glasses that are multipurpose or for wines you always drink, and then bring out the plastic tumblers for poolside or picnics.

WINE SERVING TEMPERATURE

This is a big one for me! The temperature at which you serve wine makes a huge difference. Have you ever cracked a lovely Rosé in the dead of summer and then halfway through your glass of magical wine, it suddenly doesn't taste so great? That's probably because it warmed up.

At times, proper service temperatures can literally make or break your enjoyment of wine. Here is my simple chart to follow.

If reds are too cold, they will taste thin and harsh. If reds are too warm, the alcohol will seem stronger.

If whites are too cold, you will miss the delicate aromatics, and if heavier whites (think oaked Chardonnays) are too cold you will miss nuances of the wines.

Always remember, you can stick a wine in the fridge or on ice (or take it off). A handy wine thermometer can help you check the temperature of a wine for little cost, or you can invest in a laser pointer if you want to get fancy.

SPARKLING
Serve well chilled (also important for safety in opening) at 6-10 C

LIGHT WHITES AND ROSÉS
Serve well chilled at 7-8 °C

MEDIUM TO FULL-BODIED WHITES
Serve lightly chilled at 10-13 °C

LIGHT-BODIED REDS
Serve lightly chilled at 13 °C

MEDIUM TO FULL-BODIED REDS
Serve at 15-16 °C

SWEET
Serve well chilled at 6-8 °C

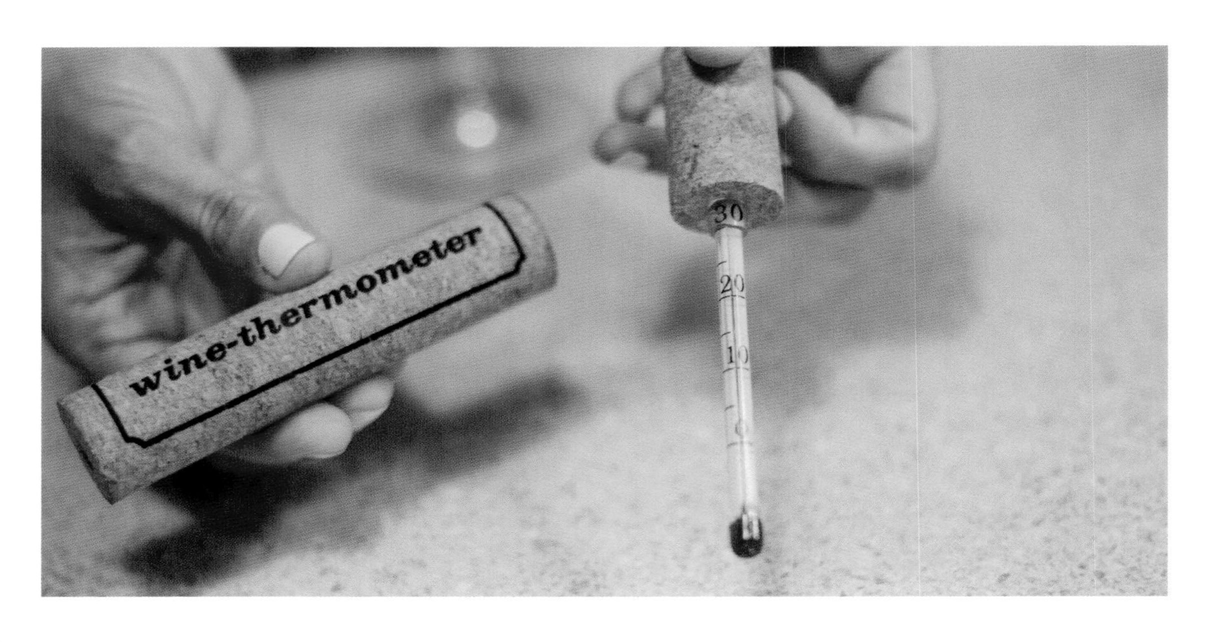

HOW TO START A WINE COLLECTION

Starting a wine cellar can seem like a daunting task but it doesn't need to be. It also doesn't need to be expensive. Here are my suggestions for success.

Storage

Consider how much space you have and how many bottles you can store as your jumping off point (and, if necessary, are you able to expand?). What's also very important is if you have the ability to store wines at proper temperature and humidity conditions. There is no point in buying expensive bottles and putting them somewhere to age that will cause them to do so prematurely. If a big built-in cellar is not for you, consider a 200-bottle temperature and humidity-controlled unit that will run you about $3K. Worth the investment in the end, especially if you end up losing expensive bottles due to poor cellar conditions.

Purchasing Wines

Ultimately, there are many ways to start a collection. This will depend on the amount you want to invest, the type of wines you like and the storage you have. Here are some of my universal truths.

1. Start small - choosing wine styles you really like to drink.

2. Explore - take those wine styles you like and find similar styles around the world. Don't be afraid to ask for help from your local Sommelier or wine shop.

3. Buy a few extra bottles and stick a small label on the back with a note of when you purchased the wine and when you should drink it. Spread out the extra bottles over a few years of drinking time so you can see how they evolve.

4. Purchase or try a few older wines (from restaurant lists, auctions, winery libraries or a friend's cellar) to explore wines with age and see how you respond to them. You may find while you like aged Bordeaux wines, you prefer younger Cabernet Sauvignons from California. Note your preferences and start ageing wines you prefer.

5. Try purchasing and organizing your cellar into 'good-better-best' so you know when you're reaching for a bottle, that you're grabbing from the right category based on the occasion.

6. Consider splitting cases of wines with friends so you don't have to commit to a 6 or 12-pack of that rare wine you can only get by the case from a wine club or a local wine agent.

7. Consider buying winery-direct. If you find a favourite producer and they ship to you, you can often become a part of their wine club and receive different and unique offerings from the winery. You can also purchase your favourites and tuck them away.

Here are some suggestions of wines that generally improve over 5-10 years of ageing in your cellar, and can cost only between $25-$50:

* Single vineyard Malbec from Mendoza, Argentina

* Dry or off-dry Riesling from Mosel or Rheingau, Germany

* Chardonnay from Oregon, USA and Ontario, Canada

* Chenin Blanc from South Africa

* Non-Vintage everyday grower Champagne

* Cabernet Franc from the Loire Valley, France

* Red Rioja Reserva from Rioja, Spain

* Late Bottle Vintage (LBV) Port from Portugal

* Cool climate Chardonnay from Ontario, Canada, Chablis, France and New Zealand

HOW TO START A WINE COLLECTION

WINES TO SPLURGE ON FOR AGING (OVER $50)

* From Burgundy, either a Chardonnay or Pinot Noir (make sure to do your research on producers)

* Classified Bordeaux

* Vintage Port

* Brunello and/or Barolo from Northern Italy

* Top Rated Champagne

* Côte-Rôtie and Hermitage reds from the Rhône Valley, France

* Cabernet Sauvignon or Bordeaux Blends from Mountain Vineyards, Sonoma and Napa Valley USA

* Syrah from Washington State, USA

Decanting Wine

I often get asked if a wine needs to be decanted, it's truthfully not always a straight-forward answer. I have seen many wines taste better after sitting on my counter opened for a day with a bit of air and other wines that haven't fared as well. Here are a few simple suggestions of when to and when not to decant.

An older wine (15 to 20 years) usually only benefits from a gentle decant as you're able to leave the sediment in the bottle and pull off the clear wine. In this case, you're not decanting to give the wine air but to not drink the sediment. To do so, leave the bottle either on its side if you have pulled it from a cellar, or stand it upright for 48 hours to allow the sediment to settle at the bottom. Carefully open the wine and gently (trying not to shake or move the bottle too much) pour the wine into a decanter (using a candle here to illuminate the neck of the bottle is helpful) and stop pouring when you have hit the sediment. This last bit of wine can be filtered through a fine filter if you like. If a wine is very old and fragile, skip the decant as it may not fair well with that much oxygen and pour straight into your glass.

Most young red wines and a few whites do benefit from decanting to aerate. Young tannic wines such as Cabernet Sauvignon, Malbec, Nebbiolo, and Shiraz will most likely 'open up' with a decant. Decanting will help tame those bold tannins and also bring forward the aromatics while helping to soften the wine. However, I have found that most young Pinot Noir also improves in the decanter after an hour or more. This is particularly true when we drink our wines a little on the young side as allowing them to breath helps to soften some of that. Surprisingly some white wines also benefit from a decant. If you're investing in a great bottle of Chablis or Chardonnay from Burgundy and they are under five years old, they will certainly be happier after an hour in a decanter (just stick the decanter on top of ice to keep the wine chilled). Play around and taste the wine at different stages of getting air, and don't rush it. Many times, I have enjoyed a wine where the last sips were the best, because they had time to receive some air.

'GREEN' WINEMAKING PRACTICES DEMYSTIFIED

Vegan-Friendly/Vegan Certified Wines

The number one diet trend in North America right now is veganism, though the term 'plant-based' is more commonly associated with the diet. True 'vegans' would refer to their choice as a lifestyle rather than a diet. Most of us would assume all wines are vegan. Fun fact: they're not. A few years ago, no one was talking about vegan wine and now it's become a huge trend with plant-based restaurants opening in record numbers and plant-based foods taking up more space on grocery shelves, and, of course, with the public becoming more informed.

Vegan-friendly wine is wine that is made without the use of any animal products or by-products in the fining or filtering of the wine, such as egg whites, fish bladder, casein or gelatin. Here, the focus is on the production process rather than what happens in the vineyard or in the packaging. Is the winery using animal manure or horses to farm? Is the bottle wax or glue for the label using animal by-products? There are many ways in which you could justifiably ask, "HOW vegan is this wine?"

Many wines being made could qualify as vegan friendly although you may need to ask the winery or winemaker to find out if your favourite brand qualifies since the labelling of wines as 'vegan-friendly' on the bottle is only now becoming more common.

While more and more winemakers are moving towards vegan practices intentionally, that's not always the case as many simply prefer to let the wine settle naturally and therefore do not need to use these fining agents. Others choose to use vegan-friendly fining agents like pea protein or plant casein among several other options. Whether intentional or not, wineries are finding more customers asking and they are more willing to promote these wines as vegan-friendly.

Vegan-Certifications

Wineries can be certified by a third-party audit and display the certification on the bottle. While this is quite new, more and more wineries are getting onboard and, interestingly, Italy and Canada are the current leaders here. Vegecert, for example, certifies that there are no animal products used in the production of the wine, but they do not certify what is happening in the vineyard or through the rest of the process or packaging.

Meanwhile in Europe, many wineries use the "V" label. The European Vegetarian Union is an organization started in 1996 in Switzerland and traditionally has identified vegetarian and vegan food. This standard, again, only looks at production. And there is an inspection and an annual fee to be a part of this organization. Interesting to note that no GMOs are allowed and there is a preference of no animal fertilizers or materials used.

Organic Wine

Organic wines have different standards based on their country of origin. And "made with organically grown grapes" refers to certified organic vineyards.

In the USA, wines are usually only made with organically grown grapes. The barrier to making full organic wine is that the rules stipulate that the wine cannot contain any additional sulphites, which arguably then makes the wine less stable once packaged.

USDA Organic certification allow no sulfites to be added during bottling to help preserve the wines. Which means wines are made with organically grown grapes, all additives (fining agents, yeast, etc) are organic, there are no GMOs (or other prohibited ingredients) or sulfur

additions (sulfites). Despite how good this all sounds, there aren't many USDA organic certified wines due to the fact that sulfur is, at the moment, the best available natural preservative for wine and so organic wines in the US can be much like natural wine. This has been a barrier for lots of winemakers when it comes to warming up to the idea of using this certification on organic wines.
Another thing to take into consideration is that grapes may be grown organically but because they are beside a vineyard that does not practice organic, they may not qualify for certification. Its important to note that around the world there are different standards for certified organic grapes and wine.

"Made with Organic Grapes"

The next step from USDA Organic is much closer to the European organic certification. These are wines made with organic grapes that also have organic additives (fining agents, yeast, etc) and have no GMOs. The one caveat to this certification is that wines are permitted to have up to 100 ppm sulfites. Because of this caveat you'll find "made with organic grapes" to be more popular with forward-thinking quality wine brands. Just so you know, this level of organic wine is not allowed the USDA Organic seal, so you'll need to seek out the words "Made with organic grapes" or "Made with organically grown grapes" on the label.

Why would a wine not be organic? Chemicals like herbicides and fungicides in vineyards can be used, and in the production of wines, other additives (like Mega Purple which is concentrated grape must used to adjust color and aroma) can be used. This type of conventional farming is concerning as these chemicals ultimately make it into the groundwater and watersheds.

Natural Wine (also known as raw wine)

Natural wine has no single definition as it really is an ideology. These wines would have the least possible intervention and the grapes used must be organic.
One could also assume all or most of the following:

* Hand-harvested grapes

* Spontaneous fermentation (no added/lab yeasts)

* No additions or adjustments (like acid, chaptalization, yeast or enzymes)

* No manipulation, micro-oxidation, or cryo-extraction

* No fining and no filtering

* Minimal or to no sulphur dioxide

* No temperature control during fermentation

* No new oak

These wines would be considered vegan-friendly as they don't use animal products in the production. Generally, these wines can display characteristics that would be considered faults in wines such as being cloudy, having sediment, or higher levels of bacteria. If you like kombucha or very natural funky beer, these wines may be for you, and they certainly do have a following.

Sustainability (or Certified Sustainable wines)

This term deals with the entire process of making wines from vine to glass and it's looking at sustainability every step of the way. While the rules of certification change from region to region, generally you can expect the following which focuses on mitigation and reduction in wastefulness and looking at the entire business model from a sustainable lens.

* Mitigation and reduction of wastefulness in winemaking

* Composting waste

* Water supply & management

* Managing pesticide and fertilizer use

* Energy use: greenhouse gas, and nitrogen use

* Economic viability

* Protection of wild-life & biodiversity on farms

* Social responsibility

* People (living wages/health benefits/access to promotion and funding towards education)

* Employee health and safety

* Winemaking: minimal intervention, indigenous yeasts, old neutral oak

* Packaging (light weight glass): are you transporting most efficiently

It is important to note that achieving a third-party audit and certification is time consuming and does cost money.

Biodynamic Wines

This term refers to an overall holistic approach at the vineyard. It is a spiritual, ethical and ecological approach to agriculture and includes organic principles plus more.

The use of natural materials, natural fertilizers and preparations replaces chemicals. And following the biodynamic calendar is another unique element to these wines. These wines and vineyards can be certified by a few organizations globally and go beyond organics into spiritual.

Based on Rudolph Steiner and Demeter Certification these would be some considerations:

* Views the farm as one living organism

* The ecosystem functions as a whole on the farm

* Breaks the tasks in the vineyard down into 4 days: Root, Flower, Fruit and Leaf days

    * Fruit days for harvesting

    * Leaf days for watering

    * Root days for pruning

    * Flower days to leave the vineyard alone!

* Calls for strange preparations such as the Cow Horn stuffed with Manure (preparation 500) but also uses nettles and chamomile

* Practices that follow the planetary constellations

* Organic: no chemical fertilizers, pesticides, or herbicides (mineral fertilizer is ok)

* Follows moon cycles for soil management, planting, cultivation, and cellar work

THANK YOU

A countless number of friends, family and industry allies have made this book possible. We are grateful to all the Canadian wineries, wine agencies and winelovers who have helped us spread the word about plant-based food & wine.

To our moms for all their support over the years and during this process, thank you.

A special thanks to Anita Dorion, for her editing eyes through this process. You are truly a social herbivore!

Thank you to the following for their support in making this book become a reality.

Amy-Louise Tracey, An Pham, Anita Adams, Anita Kapadia, Chantal Landreville, Delane Cooper, Edward Glassman, Giselle Alexander, Heather Barker, Jennifer Payette, Jill Edmonson, Jo Bennett, Katherine Huet, Kelsey, Scott and Maya Matheson McCord, Kevin Cooper, Kimberly Dobson, Laura Diane, Lenny Panzer, Linda Lee, Liz Feinstein, Margaret Weigel, Mary Baxter, Matthew Browning, Melissa Paolicelli, Melissa Stunden, Mike Twamley, Milena Brkic, MJ Shaw, Nancy Kwun, Nicole Bergot, Nicole Marchand, Peter Tymstra, Regan Macaulay, Stephanie Brown, Steve Torrens, Sunny Gandara, Vinyse Barber, Vittorio De Stefano, Vivian Rocillo, Nicole Marchand, Sunny Gandara, and Emmanuel Jal.

PRIYA RAO

A foodie and wine lover, Priya switched to a vegetarian diet in 1995 and then to a vegan one in 2011. An entertainer since childhood, she's had a lot of time to think about how to translate her love of hosting and cooking for people from meat and potatoes to vino and veggies.

Priya writes on issues around green living and vegan wine & food for Grapevine Magazine, has been a guest speaker at various vegan festivals and events and has appeared on local and national radio and television stations. These days Priya is most often found with a glass of wine in hand entertaining guests at her vegan vacation home located just outside the wine country of beautiful Prince Edward County, Ontario.

JENNIFER HUETHER, MS

Jennifer's love affair with wine started in her early twenties with taking an interest course at George Brown College in fundamentals and immediately was hooked. From there, she leapt into the Sommelier Certification from ISG, graduating top of class, then attained the Diploma of Wine from WSET, followed by the Advanced Sommelier designation in England and finally the Master Sommelier Exams-becoming Canada's first female Master Sommelier in 2011.

After winning the Ontario Sommelier Competition in 2006, Jennifer decided to invest her energy heavily in the execution of the competitions from 2008 to 2019. Along with her personal passion for plant-based food, Jennifer is passionate about promoting and uplifting all women in wine.